"Barbaro, Smarty Jones and Ruffian: The People's Horses"

By
Linda G. Hanna

Best wishes!!
Linda Hanna

Middle Atlantic Press

First Edition

1 2 3 4 5   12 11 10 09 08

Cover designed by Desiree Rappa
Interior designed by Enform Graphic Productions, Inc.

Dedication

To
Frank Y. Whiteley, Jr.
Ruffian's caregiver
Hall of Fame trainer
to a man of few words,
who taught by example,
who valued his equine charges
more than anything,
and leaves us a legacy
of honesty, diligence and care.

For
Sentell (Sonny) Taylor
a NYRA presence for over forty years,
a gracious, generous and caring person
without whom this book
would not have been possible.
You're the greatest!

For
my husband, Bob,
a special thank you
for all of your love, care and support
during the writing of this book.
For helping me to capture the charisma
of these three wonderful horses and
bring their message to everyone.
All my love.

Remembrances of friends
that passed on during the writing of this book and
who contributed to its content and completion:
Dr. Lynne Marie Maletz, John Jordan, Paul Stephens,
Shadow, Mattie, Nellie and Jenny
You will always be in my heart.

Table of Contents

THE GOVERNOR

Perhaps no other sport transfixes the attention of the nation as the five weeks in May and June during horse racing's Triple Crown. You don't have to be a regular track-going handicapper to become entranced by the drama that unfolds between the Kentucky Derby and the Belmont. This book, "The People's Horses," graphically details some of history's most gripping Triple Crown stor s—Ruffian taking on the boys in glorious fashion but ending in horrible tragedy, and Barbaro who showed such promise—perhaps a Triple Crown winner—by crushing the field in the Derby and then tragically breaking down in the Preakness. However, it was Barbaro's gallant fight for survival that gripped the nation's attention. Each week his fans, especially children, had their spirits rise and fall depending on the latest medical report. During this period, Dean Richardson, Barbaro's veterinarian, became the most famous doctor in America. Sadly, Barbaro's story also ended in tragedy.

And, as Dr. Hanna so kindly describes, Smarty Jones' trip through the Triple Crown was perhaps the most gripping of all. Smarty Jones was truly an unlikely champion—a small horse by thoroughbred standards with only average bloodlines who was trained not at one of the elite Kentucky bluegrass farms but at a working man's track, Philadelphia Park. These, however, were the characteristics that made him so popular in the Philadelphia region and throughout the nation. As he raced to victory at the Kentucky Derby and the Preakness (by a record margin of victory), the nation fell in love. That was especially true in the Philadelphia area, which was literally starved for a champion. As Smarty Jones prepared for the Belmont, people believed that his victory was assured and we would finally have another Triple Crown winner. In Philadelphia, people asked if, after the Belmont, Smarty Jones could parade down Broad Street. But, as with Ruffian and Barbaro, our hearts would break again. Despite having all the horses crowd in on him, Smarty Jones got to the top of the stretch four lengths ahead and our hearts sorared. The next furlongs seem to last forever and the agony was slow, steady, and sure as Birdstone gradually caught and passed Smarty Jones in the last 100 yards. As the race finished, an almost dead silence fell over the record crowd. In accepting the winner's trophy, Birdstone's owner apologized to the nation for denying Smarty Jones his place in history.

Amazingly, however, the love and affection did not diminish after his defeat. He received even more mail, mostly from school children around the country, saying that they were sorry and that he was still their hero.

Just as Smarty Jones lifted the nation, he did the same for horse racing. Interest in the sport boomed, and it is not an exaggeration to say that his popularity helped pass expanded gaming at race tracks in Pennsylvania.

Dr. Hanna brings all of these stories–the triumphs and the tragedies–to life in this wonderful story about three of the "people's horses."

Edward C. Randall

Patricia L. Chapman
Someday Farm
Doylestown, Pennsylvania

This book "Barbaro, Smarty Jones and Ruffian: The People's Horses" is written by a fan for other fans of racing. It celebrates the greatness of three legendary equine individuals and tells their stories, as they have never been told.

In the last few years with horses such as Smarty Jones and Barbaro, many new fans have been introduced to the "Sport of Kings." It is refreshing to have a book that looks at both the history and future of this great sport.

Today the racing industry faces many challenges. Among our spectators are those who view horse racing as cruel, and express concern about the fate of horses not as fortunate as Smarty Jones. This book addresses these issues, and many others that illuminate the strong competitive spirit and rich history of this great sport.

For the proud tradition to continue as we have known it, funds must be raised to care for retired horses, improve conditions for others and continue needed research to maintain the health of our equine charges. I am pleased to say that Linda Hanna, the author of the book, has chosen the Kentucky Equine Humane Center, as a designated charity for a portion of the book's proceeds. This recently-established effort provides rescue, placement and adoption opportunities for all breeds of horse. Even the smallest donation can make a difference in the life of an unwanted horse.

Patricia L. Chapman
August 1, 2007

Preface

Kentucky Equine
Humane Center

Kentucky Equine Humane Center

The mission of the KENTUCKY EQUINE HUMANE CENTER is to provide humane treatment and shelter while working as a clearinghouse to seek adoptive homes for all of Kentucky's unwanted equines, regardless of breed. The center is also committed to educate the public and raise awareness for responsible equine ownership so that fewer horses end up in crisis. Its goal is to work with and serve as a model for organizations with the same mission in other states: to save America's equines from inhumane treatment.

Staci Hancock
President

Quote from Staci Hancock about the progress at the Center:

Since opening our doors in April (2007), we have taken in over 100 horses. About 65% have been Thoroughbreds, either young injured horses off the track or older mares. The other 35% have been quarter horses, pleasure horses and even some mules. We have been able to place about 50% of them into good homes. As we continue to grow and become more established, our goal is to reach out to the entire state and move more horses through the Center.

Directors

Lori Nagle, Executive Director
Joan Ciampi, Vice President
S. Bud Watson, II, Treasurer,
Susan Bryson Speckert, Esq.
Arnold Kirkpatrick
Shannon Arvin, Esq.

Staci Hancock, President
Margaret Ralph
Meg Jewett, Secretary
Tom E. Daugherty, DVM
James Smith, DVM

Founders and Advisory Board

Josephine Abercrombie
Alice Chandler
Dianne Curry
Carol and Tracy Farmer
Jennie Garlington
Becky and Greg Goodman
Staci and Arthur Hancock
John Hettinger
Julia and Arnold Kirkpatrick
Margaret Jewett

Lori Kirk-Wagner
Judy and Chris McCarron
Debbie and John Oxley
Bennie Sargent
Congressman and Mrs. Ed Whitfield
Mary Lou Whitney
  and John Hendrickson
Misdee Wrigley
Kim and Nick Zito

Acknowledgements/Author's Notes

This book is unique. Rarely, if ever, will you see a book about Thoroughbred horses written by a fan. For years I have read book after book that has been written by sportswriters. There is a difference…a fan has a different focus. The perceptions are not always the same. Many times fans appreciate thoroughbred racing from a different viewpoint and for a different reason.

The impetus for this book came from a little orange cat–the book should be dubbed the "tale of the cat," or the tail…whatever. Little Smarty Jones II a feisty ginger cat was thrown from a speeding van near the Philadelphia Airport on the afternoon when Smarty Jones lost the Belmont Stakes. When rescued, he had sustained the identical head injuries of his namesake. His recovery was slow. Little Smarty had a long road to travel which eventually brought him to a meeting with his namesake in Midway, Kentucky. After that…the rest is truly history.

When I was growing up, I remember my father being very fond of the Kentucky Derby. We would be gathered for the annual event, and he would elaborate on the meaning of this classic in the whole schema of sports. I grew up with Citation, Native Dancer, Kelso, and the other stars of the forties, fifties, and sixties. Over the years I have acquired a deep appreciation for Thoroughbred racing because of these early and wonderful memories. This sport has made me a better person; it widened my horizons; it broadened my experiences. I have always loved the sport but I needed a push to the next level.

This book would not exist today if it were not for the efforts of my former pupil Rebecca Bliley Hicks, my friend Dr. Craig Goldblatt (veterinarian at Philly Park) and the great Smarty Jones. Smarty brought all of us along…if you had even a casual interest in racing, Smarty gave you a push. It was a golden time and many more people are involved in racing today because of the Smarty Effect.

This book celebrates three great stars, Ruffian, Smarty Jones and Barbaro, and their effect on the industry and those in it. All three have left their marks in very special ways, and we have learned something from their time with us. This book is a celebration of their lives but it is much more. It is intended to be an informed conscience for the typical fan, and hopefully a catalyst for the changes that are needed to save this wonderful sport. The Sport of Kings is in transition and needs to attract the same level of fan base that my Father's generation supplied. For this, they need our help, and each new step can be a beginning. Competition from off-track betting, declining purses and negative publicity have impacted racing and have had far-reaching effects. They need our help to keep this wonderful tradition alive for us and for the next generation.

A portion of the proceeds from this book will be given to The Kentucky Equine Humane Center. Horse rescue is very much a part of today's issues with slaughterhouses and the like. The folks working with Staci Hancock are doing wonderful things for the unwanted and needy horses, and they need our help.

Special thanks go to the many people who helped in the preparation of this book. I could not have accomplished any of it without my dear husband, Bob, who supported me in the long hours and short trips that were necessary for all three of these horses' stories. I could not have done it without you.

To dear friends, Laurie Johnson, Sister Patricia Spingler, I.H.M, Doreen Meier, Skip McGrath, Stephanie Kampes Lamonica, Pat McGeever, Kitty Osborn and Liza Stude, who shared my vision, endured my questions and proofread the document many times. Your insights and contributions were invaluable.

To Mrs. Patricia Chapman for sharing Smarty Jones with all of us over these past few years. For me, Pat, your insights and support made a tremendous difference in imparting the stories of these horses' lives and the messages within them.

To our Governor Edward G. Rendell–for his support of racing within the state of Pennsylvania, his efforts in saving this sport for the Keystone State and for taking the time to prepare a foreword for this book.

To Mr. Frank Y. Whiteley, Jr. for his wonderful insight, information and assistance. You have helped me in a special way to keep her wonderful legend and memory alive. God bless.

To Sentell (Sonny) Taylor, at Belmont Park, who contributed so much to this effort. Sonny, you were there for everything that I needed for this book, and helped to piece together the Ruffian puzzle–thirty-two years later. Thank you also to Ralph Theroux, Marshall Cassidy, and Stephen Foster, the other placing judges who aided me in my research.

To Deb Given, Smarty Jones's godmother, for sharing her wonderful photos and experiences from Someday Farm.

To all of my friends at Three Chimneys Farm–I could not have done it without you. To Dan Rosenberg whose thoughts and analysis were invaluable resources. To Sandy Hatfield (Smarty's stallion manager) who made innumerable calls for me, shared these wonderful horses and tolerated one million questions–I am very grateful. To Anne Peters for her wonderful insights into the pedigrees of these horses and their tremendous potential and accomplishments on the racetrack. To Ann Hayes for welcoming me on a tour and giving me a glimpse of the PR efforts generated for the entire fan base. To Margaret Layton for her efforts in the more technical aspects of this book and in securing some coveted photos for the book.

To the veterinarians of these wonderful horses. All of you helped with your professional analyses of a number of different injuries. Drs. James Prendergast and Manuel Gilman (Ruffian), Drs. Patricia Hogan, Roger Clymans and Peter Bousum (Smarty Jones), and Drs. Kathy Anderson and Dean W. Richardson

(Barbaro). Special thanks, Dr. Richardson and Dr. Bousum, for your "fan friend-ly" explanations of all of these horses' injuries.

To the SFA friends, Regina Scheerer, Joanne Bonsall, Linda Schramm and Rose Mioskie for their encouragement, support and assistance with this book.

To Gretchen Jackson, for taking me to see Barbaro at New Bolton in October 2006, and for giving me the nudge to seek a publisher for this book.

To Staci and Arthur Hancock whose passion for humane treatment of all horses has impacted this book tremendously. Thank you.

To Lynn Lifshin whose poetry on Ruffian was a real inspiration for my writ-ing.

To Bill Turner whose experience and knowledge greatly enhanced my research. Your firsthand remembrances of Ruffian and Mr. Whiteley, were a tremendous help.

To all of the Hicks—Dave, John and Rebecca, for making so many connec-tions and for providing much needed technical assistance. You were the best!

To Mike Bell, and those at Mill Ridge Farm. Mike, your insights with Ruffian were so helpful in understanding her temperament and spirit. At Mill Ridge, we brought the Barbaro family onboard. Thank you.

To all those at Claiborne farm, especially Dell Hancock and Tony Battaglia, who reviewed so much of the history and pedigrees associated with their great heritage.

To Jay Stephens, the consummate fan, for all of his support of my efforts. Without you, Jay, I would not have viewed all of their races (horse_racing@ mac.com)—it is greatly appreciated.

To those who aided my research—for Wayne Spillove, Chairman of the Pennsylvania Historical and Museum Commission, for Jeff Seder of EQB, for Cathy Schenck and Phyllis Rogers at the Keeneland Library, Sara Dorroh at Thoroughbred Times, Katherine Veitschegger at the Kentucky Derby Museum and Alex Brown of Fans of Barbaro.

To Heather Rohde (rohdefineart.com), a renowned and highly acclaimed equine artist, for her beautiful renditions of these wonderful horses.

To those who provided technical assistance—Pierre E. Bellocq for his brilliant Daily Racing Form cartoons, Michael Chapman, Don Giles, Dan Farrell, Bob and Adam Coglianese, Mike Wylot, Dell Hancock, Jennifer Duffy, Alex Brown, Three Chimneys and Paul Pugliese for valuable photos, and Mark Dietzler for working with me in bringing these wonderful photo presentations to life.

Prologue

In world literature, a "hero" is envisioned as the epitome of strength and valor, who accomplishes incredible feats in noble and compelling ways. Seeking minimal remuneration or reward, the hero (or heroine) elevates legions of followers to new and greater heights by virtue of his/her charisma.

American society today embraces its heroes, especially sports heroes. Ignorant of their faults and foibles, Americans have been known to rally around a failing team or an injured athlete more than any other country in the world. In this same vein, they relish the efforts of our four-legged animal athletes. Horseracing fans in the 1920s elevated Man O' War to the status of a national landmark. His funeral in 1947 was broadcast over radio and covered by press from all over the world. As American society struggled from the grip of the Great Depression, it celebrated the underdog Seabiscuit in his quest to upset Triple Crown winner, War Admiral at the Pimlico Special in 1938. By some people's standards, it was dubbed the greatest "sporting event" in American history. For those of another generation, there was the Great Match Race of 1975 between filly Triple Crown winner, Ruffian, and her male counterpart, Kentucky Derby-winning colt, Foolish Pleasure. Advocates of the "feminist" movement were still reeling from the upset of Bobby Riggs at the hands of Billy Jean King. Ruffian had become their newest poster child whose victory in "The Match" was almost guaranteed. Before a record-setting audience of 50,000 Belmont fans and 20,000,000 national TV viewers (the largest audience to date), Ruffian's leg snapped like a twig in the first quarter mile and her life was shattered. CBS sports announcer, Jack Whitaker, said it all, "Nothing can take away the horror of seeing a horse break down. It is like seeing a masterpiece destroyed."

Her fans represented a cross-section of American society from girl scouts to grandmothers and nuns to truck drivers. After thirty-two years, her death does not rank up there with the assassination of President John F. Kennedy or the invasion of Pearl Harbor, but there are thousands of people who could tell you where they were when they heard the news about Ruffian. In the record books, she is an undefeated queen never headed or beaten in any race which she finished. In each stakes or champion race, she either equaled or set a new track record. Although the near black equine shooting star passed, her memory has not.

Almost thirty years passed before another equine super star, Smarty Jones, would win the public's hearts and become America's horse. To make the story more interesting, the colt departed from Kentuckiana tradition and was Pennsylvania-born and bred. In somewhat of a Seabiscuit repeat, the Chapmans self undefeated and knocking on the door of Churchill Downs in one of the most exciting Derbies of the last fifty years. Following in the footsteps of his relative, Seattle Slew, Smarty was the first undefeated Derby winner to make the trip to Pimlico since 1977. In his pursuit of the Triple Crown, Smarty Jones rocked the entire nation ... even making the trip from Philadelphia to New York for the Belmont Stakes in a police motorcade. To date, everyone who followed Smarty to any degree knows the outcome of that sad day at Elmont, New York, when Smarty lost his race by a length and we lost our star with a career-ending injury.

That was 2004, and Smarty Mania is still alive and well in the USA. Legions of fans make the pilgrimage to visit Smarty in Midway, Kentucky, in a tour that is booked months in advance. In the early days of 2008, ninety-three more little Smarties will hit the tracks running as they graduate from race track school.

This past year at the 2006 Derby, another undefeated horse challenged a very talented field and won dramatically in the largest margin of victory in sixty years. Once again Americans, fastening their seat belts for the roller coaster ride of May and June, looked to the ghosts of Triple Crowns' past and the charisma of Barbaro for redemption. Could this be the horse that everyone was waiting for?

Every conceivable statistic from Barbaro's short career had been analyzed, and the hype-levels were off the meter as the Preakness Stakes at Pimlico on May 20 approached. Through the media, the public relived the heroics of Barbaro's trainer, Michael Matz, who had rescued three children from a burning plane in an Iowan cornfield a decade before, and the anguish of Barbaro's jockey, Edgar Prado, who had exhausted all efforts to save his dying mother from the ravages of cancer. Owners of Barbaro, Gretchen and Roy Jackson, knowing that life would not be "normal" for sometime, graciously related the highlights of a thirty-year involvement with thoroughbred horses from their West Grove, Chester County, Pennsylvania farm. The flourish continued until it was finally race day. Then in the blink of an instant.....all tranquility and promise were destroyed right before our eyes, as Barbaro's right hind foot and ankle dangled before TV cameras around the world.

To date, there are very few people who could not relate the outcome of this gut- wrenching ordeal. The nation became totally absorbed in the daily struggle of Barbaro, the valiant fighter. In the early days of his recuperation he had outlasted the naysayers, who believed it wasn't possible to bring a horse back from this level of injury. Over the next 254 days, Barbaro would struggle to beat the odds with the nation rooting for him. After many successes, the law of averages kicked in and he could not rally against the laminitis that plagued him with insurmountable odds. The wise care-givers, who loved him ever so much, made the decision to rid him of the shackles that had become too much to bear. He left us with a legacy of caring, wisdom and love. As Ruffian and Smarty before, he became our hero....he had fought the good fight and had given his all.

RUFFIAN

"She was one of those rare flashes of brilliant light that shines so brightly for so short a time yet is not forgotten." - Jennifer Oltmann

Horseracing in the 1970s

The sport of thoroughbred horseracing experienced somewhat of a "renaissance" during the 1970s. Many have called it the Golden Age of modern racing with the emergence of so many superstars. With the dazzling exploits of Secretariat and the elusive Triple Crown, the thrill of horseracing had returned and in a "big" way. In the wake of Secretariat, other dynamic stars took center stage; among them were Seattle Slew, Affirmed, Alydar, Exceller, Forego and Spectacular Bid.

It seemed that after a twenty-five year drought, Triple Crown winners had become a dime-a-dozen. Within a five-year period America would christen three in the victories of Secretariat (1973), Seattle Slew (1977) and Affirmed (1978). These horses were outstanding in their performance, but radiating above all of them was another real jewel, Ruffian. She was a queen in her own right and had captured the Filly Triple Crown in 1975, a feat that had been accomplished only three times before. Not too many people will question that Ruffian might be the greatest filly ever; some may even suggest that she may have been greater than Secretariat himself. Unfortunately, the fates have denied us the time to make any more than a conjecture.

During the 1970s, the country found itself in a bit of an economic and political depression. After years of frustration with the Vietnam War, factions within the country were at odds with each other. The fallout from the surrender of South Vietnam loomed large on the horizon, and the economy offered no safe haven as it slid on a collision course toward recession. Feeling thwarted on all sides, the sports public welcomed the pleasant distraction that these wonderful racing stars provided.

For those who saw Ruffian, she was the epitome of equine perfection. She was tall, stately and regal with legs that seemed to go on forever. She became *The Black Beauty* or *The Black Stallion* of our childhood dreams with a heart larger than life. As her jockey Jacinto Vasquez expressed, "She was like Marilyn Monroe or Raquel Welsh walking into a room," she took your breath away. With all of this, her talents seemed to know no bounds. She was undefeated in every race that she finished and either equaled or broke the track record. It was no wonder that the entire nation, most of whom had never watched a horse race or placed a bet, was taken with her, as she became a Superwoman on four legs.

Even the sportswriters had a field day with her accomplishments. As CBS Sports news writer Bud Morgan said, "She just stood out in looks, temperament and attitude…there was nothing ordinary about this horse at all." Following suit, Frank Deford from *Sports Illustrated* wrote, "She was monstrous and as game an athlete as you could possibly ever expect…a creature beyond Pegasus himself." Knowing her business when she arrived at the track, she set out to dismiss her competition and stride to the winner's circle. In everything that she did, she was perfect. Who could have ever imagined that such perfection would end in such tragedy?

The Filly's Inner Circle

In American thoroughbred horse racing, the perfect formula for continued success seems to be to "breed the best to the best." This is the loftiest of ambitions, which may for one reason or another fall short of its goal. With the marriage of Mr. and Mrs. Henry Carnegie Phipps's daughter, Barbara, to Stuart Janney, Jr. in 1936, two wonderful equine traditions were united whose success in thoroughbred racing would be guaranteed for years to come.

Barbara Phipps Janney's family was one of the most successful within the industry. Her mother, Gladys Phipps, had been one of the most prominent breeders in America. It was from Mrs. Phipps's Wheatley Stable that the classic winner and leading sire Bold Ruler emerged, and would go on to sire the great Secretariat. Mrs. Janney's brother Ogden Phipps was a successful owner and chairman of The Jockey Club.

The Janney family members were also long-standing horse enthusiasts. As an amateur steeplechase rider, Stuart Janney, Jr. had won the Maryland Hunt Club Cup four times during the '30s and '40s by traversing a challenging four miles over timber and through woodland. As a grandson of the former Governor of Maryland, Stuart Janney's roots in the state ran deep. At the time of their marriage, the couple purchased the 400 acre Locust Hill Farm in Glyndon, Maryland. They began breeding thoroughbred horses by the '50s. From the beginning, their focus for Locust Hill Farm was to be a smaller farm that bred judiciously and sought quality at all times.

The trainer for many of the Locust Hill Farm horses was Frank Y. Whiteley, Jr., a plainspoken but highly experienced horseman. Some considered him to be conservative in nature but he cared a great deal about the animals within his charge. A native of Maryland's Eastern Shore, the sinewy and white-haired Whiteley had cut his eyeteeth in the business. At the age of six he acquired his first horse from his father. Thus began a career with horses that would span more than sixty years. In the beginning, Whiteley worked the "frying pan and leaky-roof circuit" of minor tracks with cheap horses, usually running the forgotten ones against the unknowns, and was paid peanuts for his efforts. To keep things afloat, he would groom the horses and muck the stalls.

Working his way up within the business, Whiteley conditioned several divisional champions. The first of these was Raymond R. Guest's Tom Rolfe, son of Ribot. The colt had won stakes races as a two year old but his best season was 1965. In Tom Rolfe, Whiteley saddled his first Kentucky Derby entrant, who took a disappointing third behind Lucky Debonair and Dapper Dan. Later Tom Rolfe went on to be the 1965 Champion Three Year Old and winner of the Preakness Stakes, Arlington Classic, Citation Handicap, Chicagoan Stakes and the American Derby among others. It was quite an accolade for a Maryland farm boy, but Whiteley seemed unaffected by the whole thing.

It was only two years later that Whiteley acquired another Horse of the Year Award. This time it was with Damascus, son of Sword Dancer, who was owned by Mrs. Thomas Bancroft. Damascus had captured the Preakness and Belmont Stakes. Later in the Woodward, he defeated Buckpasser and Dr. Fager by 10 lengths. Unfortunately in the Kentucky Derby, however, Whiteley would once again send out the third-place finisher as Damascus's rally stalled in the stretch. Years later when given a choice, Whiteley avoided the Kentucky Derby for Ruffian. This decision was framed by his past experiences with Tom Rolfe and Damascus.

Another success story for Whiteley was the great Forego. In 1976, he took over the conditioning of the 1974 and 1975 Horse of the Year for Martha Gerry, his owner and breeder. The great gelding, despite an array of physical problems, went on to win the Metropolitan Mile, the Brooklyn Handicap and the Woodward Handicap. Perhaps the greatest of his tests in 1976 was winning the Marlboro Cup as he carried an Atlas-like weight of 137 pounds. This effort helped to cement another Horse of the Year honor and he would return in 1977 to defend his title. Whiteley seemed to have that special touch to bring out the best in each of his charges.

To those who knew Whiteley on a personal level, he was quiet, shrewd and uncompromising. He was nicknamed the "fox of Laurel," by those who knew him well. The press and its contingent were intruders of the first order, and Whiteley thought nothing of sending them with their photographers to the wrong stall just to be ornery. He knew his business, and didn't wish to be bothered while he was trying to do it.

His employees regarded him highly and thought twice before they would disregard his wishes. One of his assistant trainers was Mike Bell, who commented on his years with Whiteley:

It was a very rewarding experience to be part of Frank Whiteley's operation. It's funny but when you read about some of the people who trained thoroughbreds fifty, seventy-five years ago, you can see a lot of Mr. Whiteley in them. It was always about the horses. The money's important, but the horses have to come first. He was one of the last of the 'old school' trainers, and when he retired it was sort of like the end of an era.

For those who knew him at Belmont Park, he was a constant in the industry. One of the Placing Judges, Sentrell (Sonny) Taylor, who has been there for over forty years, remembers him this way:

Frank Whiteley was an amazing man. He was here at 4:30 in the morning....When he ran a horse, he would stand right down there by the winner's circle, watch the horse run and then, when the horse was unsaddled, he was right behind. He didn't sit up in the stands with the owners; he wasn't a club house trainer. He was an old-fashioned trainer...He trained flat horses and jumpers, and he trained steeplechase horses, too.

Over the years, Whiteley had assumed the role of a chieftain with his employees. Like many good horse professionals, he enjoyed horses more than people. He was protective of his horses and would accept nothing other than perfection from his staff. In addition to his many horse charges, Frank Whiteley trained many future trainers by his example. It wasn't about what he said; it was what he did and how he did it. Some of those who worked for him, and went on to be very successful trainers include: Mike Bell, Claude R. "Shug" McGaughey, Steve Penrod, Tom Skiffington, Charles Hadry, Al Quanbeck and Barclay Tagg. One of his assistants, Steve Penrod remembered,

I do most everything the way that I learned from him. The way I feed is the way he feeds....Pretty much about everything I do with a horse is very similar to what he did with his horses...He was very patient. He'd have horses in training a long time before they ever ran....His whole life is with the horses, and I think he really knew his horses as individuals....He's there all of the time.

The Whiteley staff consisted of some of the most devoted grooms and exercise riders. By his very nature, Frank Whiteley wouldn't have it any other way.

One of the first people that Ruffian met at Whiteley's farm was Dan Williams, a stocky man who would be her groom. Years later, Dan recalled the first day that they met, "She impressed me right away. She was just a different horse. She was *all* horse. Looked like nothin' you ever saw. The spirit of her." From the very beginning, they had a special kind of bond that would last for Ruffian's short lifetime. As Ruffian's trainer, Whiteley escorted her on his pony to and from her morning workouts, and soaked her feet in cold water when it was over. He was devoted to her in every way and better than anyone else understood her frightening speed. When the jockeys mounted before the race, the directions were simple, "Don't get her hurt and don't get her beat."

Other members of Ruffian's stable family included exercise riders, Yates Kennedy, Squeaky Truesdale and Charlsie Cantey. Over those few years, a number of riders would have the privilege of exercising Ruffian, or "Sofie" as she was called in the stable. To sit on Ruffian was like relaxing on a large soft sofa; hence, she acquired her nickname. Years later Cantey would remember Ruffian, "She was big, but a nice filly. Ruffian was no problem. She was practically bulletproof then."

As Ruffian grew larger and stronger, she strutted her stuff. She was a very muscular horse, and even Yates Kennedy, who weighed at least 130 pounds, could tell you that riding her and pulling her up were no small chores. She would do well in the hands of an experienced jockey, and Frank Whiteley knew someone with the same kind of fighting spirit that Ruffian had. His choice was Jacinto Vasquez.

When Vasquez was thirteen, he left his family's farm in Panama. Being one of ten children and dirt poor had put him on the streets, and before long he found himself in trouble with the law. He had been arrested after a nasty street fight. When he was about to be jailed, a woman intervened. She promised to take care of him and keep him out of trouble. The woman was well known as the owner of an open-air market nearby, so the policeman relented. As it turned out, Mrs. Gustines was the mother of a famous Panamanian Jockey, Heliodoro Gustines. That Sunday, she took Jacinto to the racetrack to find him a job. After working his way up in the ranks, he began riding horses during workouts or races. Before long, he was brought to the United States and the rest is history.

When Vasquez got the chance to ride Ruffian for the first time, he took her for a workout. They left the gate and after a quarter mile he tried to pull her up. She was bent on going faster and faster; it took all of his strength to slow her pace. Recalling that day many years later, Vasquez said, "I never run a horse like that. She was a horse that knew what she was doing. She was all horse, when she run that first time."

When Whiteley first laid eyes on Ruffian he said, "She was a grand-looking filly." A little later on he would take her to the track, watch her go around and clutch his stopwatch. Then with a tight-lipped smile, he would say, "She's some filly." At that point she was unnamed and referred to as the Reviewer filly or the Shenanigans filly, because of her sire and dam. She came from a long line of regal and successful thoroughbreds, but her story had yet to be written.

Regal Lineage

Each year as a birthday gift from her mother, Mrs. Barbara Janney received a free season, which translated to a mare of her choosing being bred to one of her mother's best studs, usually Bold Ruler. Unfortunately Bold Ruler fell ill and would have to be euthanized, so in 1971, Barbara, or Bobbie as she was called, bred her mare Shenanigans to one of Bold Ruler's sons, Reviewer. Ruffian was the result of this union.

It was customary for the Janneys to keep several of their horses at Claiborne Farm, in Paris, Kentucky. It was there in the late evening hours of April 17, 1972, that Ruffian was foaled. She was a large and near black (dark bay) filly with a white star on her forehead. Her heritage would suggest that she was touched with greatness, and the star on her head was only an indication of what was yet to come.

The Janneys were pleased with the newest addition to the Locust Hill Farm, and gave her a name that had been reserved for a colt, which they had previously sold. The baby filly was to be called Ruffian. "Girls can be ruffians, too," Barbara Janney explained. In retrospect, the name complemented Ruffian's demeanor, for she was large, tough, dominant and self-possessed.

Everything in Ruffian's pedigree suggested greatness. The Janneys had acquired Bold Irish (by Fighting Fox-a full brother to Triple Crown winner Gallant Fox) from Barbara's mother, Mrs. Phipps. In 1960, Bold Irish produced the Janneys' first stakes winner, Knocklofty. Bearing the red and white colors of Locust Hill, Knocklofty had captured the Prince George and Annapolis stakes — two races reserved for Maryland-bred horses.

As one of the Janneys three original mares from Mrs. Phipps, Bold Irish was a foundation mare at Locust Hill. In 1962, she was bred to Native Dancer. He was television's first notable horse because of his gray color, which stood out on the black-and-white screens of the 1950s. Known for his brilliant come-from-behind style, Native Dancer had only failed once. That was in his bid for the Kentucky Derby, where he came in second. Many who watched the race believed that his failure was due to the jockey's poor judgment, and he was denied the Triple Crown title that he rightly deserved. It was Native Dancer's gray daughter, Shenanigans, out of Bold Irish, who would live up to her pedigree through her offspring, little black filly Ruffian. On the track, Shenanigans had won only 3 of 22 starts, but she was already the dam of Icecapade, a multiple stakes winner. It was Icecapade who would later sire the "Iron Lady," Lady's Secret.

On the Phipps's side was the renowned Bold Ruler who had sired the great Secretariat of Triple Crown fame. The baby filly Ruffian was a granddaughter of Bold Ruler, her father being Ogden Phipps's Reviewer, another of Bold Ruler's speedy sons. Reviewer had been impressive enough on the racetrack by winning 9 out of 13 starts, but he seemed to be plagued with injuries. After three cannon bone fractures, he was permanently retired. Ruffian was among the first crop of foals sired by Reviewer.

There are many who believe that Reviewer never lived up to his pedigree. As a grandson of Nasrullah, and a great-grandson of Nearco, he showed the same degree of promise that his sire Bold Ruler had, but seemed to fall short in the final analysis. While Bold Ruler had been a capable enough runner, his greater success rested in the breeding shed. As leading sire for eight years (seven consecutive ones), he sired eleven champions, among them the two-time Horse of the Year, Secretariat.

While Ruffian was to be the greatest of the Janney-Whiteley success stories, there were many others. The Janneys had access to many of the sought-after stallions in the country, as well as some very desirable bloodlines within their own family circle.

Early Lessons

At Claiborne Farm, Ruffian spent her first six months with her dam Shenanigans and the other fillies and mares. During these months, the young filly grew strong and healthy in preparation for the next stage in her progression to become a racehorse one day. As was the custom at Claiborne, the fillies were separated from their dams on a certain day in October, known as "weaning day." This same tradition did not exist at most other farms, which separated the fillies from the dams according to age and in a more gradual fashion. For Ruffian and the other young fillies, it was a frightening experience with small emotional wounds that time would quickly heal. For the dams, many of whom had been through this before, it was a matter of natural course.

When the doors of the large van finally opened, the frightened fillies found themselves in a completely different stall with nice clean hay and plenty of good food to eat. In a few days, they would forget their other life, and spend more time outside running and playing through the long and cold winter. During this time at Raceland Farm, on the other side of Paris, Ruffian would learn the early rudiments of being a racehorse. It was critical that she learn to accept a saddle, bit and rider before moving onto the training stable at Xalapa.

In a natural progression of events, the stable hands would arrive every morning and fasten a wide strap over her back and under her belly. She tried many times to shake it loose and it would not give. This strap, known as a surcingle, held the saddle and after a while, Ruffian didn't seem to know that it was there. Before too long, a small boy would come and lay across the saddle as Ruffian was being led around. Gradually she would become accustomed to the weight and the turning left or right, when there was a slight pull on the side of her mouth. These lessons were of vital importance in conditioning her to accept a rider who would sit on her back with his feet in the stirrups and his hands on the reins.

After ten long months of adjustment, Ruffian was ready to make another move from Raceland to the training stable known as Xalapa. There she would learn how to behave as a racehorse, but not necessarily how to run. That would come later. One day, a gentleman named Nicholas Lotz arrived to exercise the yearlings. He had broken Ruffian's half-brother, Icecapade, and was very interested in the new Shenanigans filly. Lotz was later to recall, "Ruffian had a huge girth. Usually you would use a girth that was forty inches long, maybe forty-two. But for Ruffian, we had to get a girth that was forty-eight inches long. She was a big filly, and fine-boned, too."

Within a week Lotz was able to straddle Ruffian and guide her in circles and figure eights within her stall. It is important for the horse to follow the rider's lead. She must become accustomed to his legs and other body movements, which would direct her when she was outside. When this was accomplished, the yearlings would then work in sets while learning to line up and to turn. The riders would never ask for speed; some of the yearlings would move out in a slow trot then on to a canter.

During these months Ruffian responded well to all of Lotz's instruction. Sometimes she would lead and other times be content to follow. She singled herself from the others by her size and her ways. She was smart and she was ready to run. Her size and maturity seemed to set her apart from her peers. " I always thought Ruffian was something special, but you can't always tell. Sometimes you have a horse that is really good as a yearling, but then all of the others will catch up six months later," Lotz reflected.

The man, waiting to see if the others would catch up, was Frank Whiteley. He was the one chosen by the Janneys, to see if Ruffian was all that she appeared to be. Their first meeting took place in October 1973 near the end of her time at Xalapa. Whiteley's first recollections were, "She was a grand-looking filly. You couldn't help but like her." Well, soon enough the grand-looking filly was in a large van and off to Whiteley's barn in Camden, South Carolina.

The reputation of Frank Yewell Whiteley, Jr. had preceded him. He was known as a conservative manager with great attention to detail. His procedures were methodical, and the horse's welfare was a number one priority. He never believed in rushing them, but had a keen eye for talent and promise. It did not take very long to ascertain that Ruffian had both.

Over the winter months, Whiteley and Dan Williams her groom would walk her around for hours. Then came the "ponying," when Whiteley got on his pony and would take Ruffian's halter and lead strap and let her do an easy gallop, while he rode beside. Then before too long it was time to let her run. The instructions to the exercise boy were always specific, "Once easy," Whiteley would say, " I know she's fast, but don't let her run out. Keep her under wraps." With a stopwatch in his hand, Whiteley would watch her graceful body coast by, as if she were floating above the track. It was so effortless and so smooth. When it was over, Whiteley would glance at his watch, smile to himself and say nothing. She was almost ready...Whiteley knew it, and so did Ruffian.

Two things that Frank Whiteley looked for in a horse were "heart" and "class." They weren't something to be put on paper; it was more like a feeling, a look in their eye. Not all horses were smart either. These qualities could be seen and felt; it was a way of carrying themselves and giving all to winning. When Whiteley saw Ruffian, he knew she had it all. Now it was time to let the rest of the world in on the secret.

Two Year Old Successes

By the early spring of 1974, it was time for Whiteley to pack up his operation and return to Belmont Park. All of the staff and stable hands would make the trip up to New York just for the racing season. It was Whiteley who preferred the climate of South Carolina so much more than Florida, for it afforded the range of three different seasons, without the harshness of northern winters. He believed that it was good for the horses, and after all, the horses came first in Whiteley's book.

After careful examination of the racing schedule, he selected May 22nd for Ruffian's Maiden Race. It was to be a short distance, five and a half furlongs or less than three-quarters of a mile. The time was right, the distance was right and the jockey needed to be right, too. For this task, he chose Jacinto Vasquez who at the time was considered one of the top ten jockeys in the country. He was just thirty years old.

At Belmont Park, the New York bettors are a rare breed. They scrutinize the racing sheets, check the odds and weigh their options. The day of Ruffian's Maiden may have been the only time that the real horseplayers were caught off-guard. That was the way Whiteley hoped it would be. At that time, Ralph Theroux, a current NYRA Placing Judge, was walking toward the paddock and he remembered seeing Ruffian for the very first time.

There was this big, beautiful black filly–gorgeous. She took your breath away. I saw Yates walking along side of her, and I said, "Who is that?" And he said, "This is Ruffian, and she is running in the next race." "Do you like her?" I asked, and he said "She's something special." That was the first time that I laid eyes on her, and she was something to behold.

By waiting until the very last minute, Vasquez was able to bring her right out, bypassing the paddock all together. Not knowing how she would react to the total scene, Whiteley chose not to take any chances. But Ruffian was cool, calm and collected; it was as if she knew exactly what she was supposed to do. As Vasquez recalled, "She was a horse that knew what she was doing."

As they approached the starting gate, Ruffian acted as though she had been racing for years. She was in the number nine position, near the outside. As the gate opened, she broke a little slowly, but then surged ahead. Her personality seemed to change right before Vasquez's eyes, and she became a warrior that exploded into action. She finished fifteen lengths ahead of the other fillies, and never looked back.

Her speed in the race was staggering as she tied the record for Belmont Park. One sportswriter called it, "the greatest race ever run by a first-time starter." What he may have forgotten to note, the starter was not a colt but a filly. For the bettors going forward, this would be the only race in Ruffian's life that she was not considered the favorite.

After Ruffian's first race, Whiteley made somewhat of a quantum leap and chose to enter her in a stakes race. The Fashion Stakes was also at Belmont, and had been named in honor of a famous mare, that had defeated her male rival back in 1842. It was the first stakes race of the season for two-year-old fillies and promised a good field. Trainer MacKenzie Miller's two-year-old filly Copernica was coming from two strong wins, and their meeting in the Fashion promised some real excitement. Another undefeated filly, Jan Verzal, who was a proven stakes winner, would join their company. The Fashion was listed with a field of six strong entrants.

Starting from post position three, Ruffian was led into the starting gate behind Copernica in the second stall. That would be the closest that the two fillies would ever be. Copernica had only one eye, but that was enough to see that she was being outclassed by the confident Ruffian. When the race was over, Ruffian had won by six and a half lengths and had broken the Fashion Stakes' record. To some it seemed that Copernica had lost some of her fight after that race. It's something not easily explained, but sometimes good horses don't bounce back after a heavy loss. On the other hand, Ruffian had proved to all of the skeptics that her Maiden was not a "fluke," and she was a force to be reckoned with throughout that summer of 1974.

As Whiteley prepared Ruffian for the Astoria Stakes at Aqueduct, there were new challenges in the mix. For the first time, Ruffian would be transported to a different track and possibly a different racing surface. Her regular jockey Vasquez was serving a ten- day suspension and would have to be replaced. There was no real reason to believe that the surface would be a problem, but the change in rider could be another story. After some thought, Whiteley chose to substitute Vince Bracciale, Jr., an inexperienced but promising young jockey.

In her two previous wins, Ruffian had hesitated in leaving the gate and was forced to compensate for it in the next ten strides or so, until she charged to the front. It had not caused a problem before, but who could predict what it could mean later. If anything it was the only weakness that could be determined in two flawless appearances.

Word had gotten out and Ruffian only had three challengers in the Astoria Stakes. The other owners were beginning to recognize her dominance, and thought better of exposing their young fillies to such a commanding presence on the track. The three who chose to accept the challenge were formidable in their own right.

Ruffian broke from the gate cleanly, and strode to the lead. The jockey Bracciale let her establish her own rhythm, and she blazed to her best first quarter-mile yet in :21 4/5. With very little urging, she cleared the other horses and won by nine lengths. During this, her third race, she had carried more weight than before but her times were getting better. She had become a trainer's dream.

Coming off of her dominance in the Astoria, Ruffian was the heavy favorite going into the Sorority Stakes at Monmouth Park, her first Grade I race. She had established herself in her first three contests, and once again some of the competition chose to pass up the race. Among the brave ones was Dan Lasater's Hot 'n' Nasty, who was becoming one of the year's best performers with her undefeated record. Although Hot 'n' Nasty had a proven stakes record, the Monmouth faithful were betting on Ruffian at odds of 3-10.

As the race began Ruffian made a clean break, unlike Hot 'n' Nasty who seemed to stumble out of the gate. In the first quarter mile, Hot 'n' Nasty kept pushing Ruffian and proved to be more of a challenge than had been anticipated. The two were neck-and-neck as the pair turned into the stretch, a feat that had never happened before. As Vasquez realized what was happening and went to his whip a half a dozen times in the stretch, Ruffian responded to his effort and with a burst of speed, charged ahead of her rival. She defeated Hot 'n' Nasty by two and one-quarter lengths, bringing her record to four perfect finishes and setting another stakes record for the Sorority.

It was very unusual for the tight-lipped Frank Whiteley to openly discuss any of his horses, but he did comment on Ruffian's performance after the Sorority. Whiteley told Don Zamarelli of the *Blood-Horse*,

Ruffian's a big, strong, easy-running horse. She's fast enough to frighten the hell out of me-has been since we picked her up. From the beginning, we said she would be something special and now she's showing it. God is she! Look at the hindquarter, that is where she gets that thrust from, but you would never know it, she has such an easy way of going.

At the very end of the race Jacinto Vasquez had felt some concern about Ruffian's performance. Although there was no indication of a problem at the beginning of the Sorority, Ruffian was having trouble with a small splint. This was not discovered until several days after the race. Injuries of this nature can be common with young thoroughbreds, and they respond well to treatment and rest. Her next scheduled race was the Spinaway in Saratoga a month later. If all went according to plan, she would be ready.

After a month of rest and treatment Ruffian seemed to be back to her old self. Whiteley was concerned that she be 100% or she wouldn't be going up to the "spa," as they called it. Everyone from Belmont had made the trip but Whiteley swore up-and-down that he wouldn't venture up there a minute too soon. The press had become overbearing and he didn't like this "new-found popularity," of having his horses bothered in their stalls. He was polite but that was about as good as it got.

The Spinaway was set for Friday, August 23, the last day of a four-week-long meet. When Whiteley finally brought Ruffian up it was Tuesday. That would give the filly time to adjust to the deeper racing surface, and time for Whiteley to replace Vasquez who was out on another suspension. It had been Vince Bracciale, Jr. who had filled in the last time at the Astoria, and Whiteley had been pleased with his handling of the filly.

Ruffian broke well from number two post position and forged to the lead. The other three fillies were not serious threats per se, but Bracciale wanted to finish first without working Ruffian too hard. During the last sixteenth of a mile he pulled her up to a modest gallop, a feat that took all of his strength. No one was more surprised than he to see a time of 1:08 3/5 — a new stakes record for the Spinaway! For all of his efforts at slowing Ruffian down, she had won by thirteenth lengths. Ironically this was the same margin that her groom had predicted to the press that morning.

Her supporters were out in full force and Ruffian had not disappointed anyone with her stellar performance. Secretariat's trainer, Lucien Laurin remarked, "As God is my judge, she might be better than Secretariat." This was high praise indeed, and there would be more coming from the media as Ruffian prepared for an exciting fall campaign. Meanwhile, those speculating about the up-and-coming Eclipse Award for the Best Juvenile Filly didn't have to look any farther than the large, black, superfilly Ruffian.

As a two-year-old, Ruffian had accomplished a great deal. She had done a beautiful job at six furlongs and had surely outclassed her local competition. What Whiteley wanted for her at this point was more experience, and he set his mind on the upcoming Frizette Stakes on September 26. Little did he know at that point, that it was not in the cards for Ruffian.

On the morning of the 26th, Whiteley arrived at the barn at five o'clock only to find that Ruffian had not finished her food. After more careful scrutiny it seemed that she had a fever, sweat on her flanks and a drooping head. After a call to the racing secretary, to scratch her from the race, Whiteley called the Janneys. They were disappointed but knew that it was the right thing to be done. The horse came first.

By the next day, the fever was gone, but things just didn't seem right. Whiteley watched Ruffian move in her stall, and she appeared to miss a step. After bringing her out and all around, she seemed to be perfectly okay. The next day it happened again and Whiteley had seen enough. He sent for Dr. Prendergast, a track veterinarian, who was asked to do x-rays of her hindquarters and legs. After one hundred films the vet couldn't find anything amiss, but Whiteley persisted. After sending the pictures down to Dr. Alex Harthill in Kentucky a diagnosis was made. Ruffian had a hairline fracture in her right pastern. She would require a cast for about six weeks and stall rest.

After conferring with Whiteley, Harthill took the next plane up and fashioned a plaster of Paris cast for Ruffian. All would be fine if the filly tolerated the cast. It took Ruffian about two hours to make a statement as she kicked a dent into the cast. They quickly replaced it with a jelly cast which could be changed every few days. The human caregivers knew what was best for Ruffian, but she was running the show and would have none of it. More than ever it was clear to Whiteley that she would need her stall rest, and that stall would be in Camden, South Carolina–away from all of the hype and confusion. When interviewed, he told the *Blood-Horse*, "Got here last week, just keeping her in the stall, maybe a couple more weeks…Don't think that break amounts to much."

The end-of-the-year awards brought the Eclipse Award for the Best Juvenile Filly, and there were no surprises there. The Janneys were unable to make the trip to San Francisco so Whiteley went in their place. It was his sixtieth birthday and the filly's win was very special, although Frank Whiteley would never admit it to anyone. He was high on this horse, but most times he kept his comments to himself.

Better Than Ever

As spring came around, it was time to consider the move back up to Belmont. The filly was feeling fine, and her times were showing that she hadn't lost any of her spirit. When they would be back in New York, she would need a serious workout at Belmont and then she would need a race. On April 13th she got her three-furlong gallop in: 34 and Whiteley was more than satisfied with her condition. In a very clever move he placed her name in an overnight allowance race the next day. To say the competition wasn't overly thrilled would be an understatement. Two owners gave a few words to the media, "We're not very smart, but we're brave," announced Viola Sommer, whose Witty Ways was another of the entrants. And John A. Morris, owner of Channelette, told the *Blood-Horse*, "I felt I had been led into deep waters." These words were somewhat of a prediction as Ruffian pulled away from every other horse to win by four and three-quarter lengths. The real Ruffian was back; she was good and she knew it. At the end of the race, any race, she would parade to the Winner's Circle to receive her public. She would have her ears up and a cocky way about her, as much as to say, "Did you see what I just did?"

With the filly back and feeling fit, Whiteley announced that her next scheduled race would be the Comely Stakes. This race was significant because it served as a precursor to the Filly Triple Crown races– the Acorn, the Mother Goose and the Coaching Club American Oaks. This was a distinguished series which Whiteley and the Janneys were committed to attempt.

The Comely was run at Aqueduct where Ruffian had eclipsed the Astoria. It was a seven-furlong race that took place three days before the Run for the Roses. The event had attracted a field of five with Ruffian the favorite at odds of 1-20. Ruffian broke poorly but quickly compensated for her shortcoming. Several challenged, but no one horse could get an upper hand on Ruffian. She finished ahead by seven and three-quarter lengths at 1:21 1/5, which was a second off of the track record. With very little effort she had set another new stakes record. Her jockey recalled, "She came back perfectly after the injury. She was perfect. Each race she ran better than the one before."

When Ruffian had first made her mark at Belmont Park, NYRA veterinarian, Manuel Gilman gave his assessment of her:

> After two races, I recognized that she was something extraordinary. As far as her physical make-up was concerned, she was much larger than the average filly; as a matter of fact, she was larger than the average colt. In her third year,

she weighed 1125 pounds. She never looked large, because she was so well proportioned…She was a very healthy filly, with a very long stride. She never looked like she was going as fast as she was. This particular filly was the best that had been around in many generations if not the best ever.

It wasn't a secret that Ruffian's dominance was keeping many of the up-and-coming filly stars away from her races. A few like Copernica appeared to lose some of their charge after being blown away by the big black bullet. Many track photographers claimed that Ruffian had to be ignored in many of their photos in order to capture the second and third place horses.

Some of the naysayers were waiting for Ruffian's Achilles' heel to come to the fore. There had to be something that she couldn't do well. After all, she wasn't perfect, or was she?

The Filly Triple Crown

With this seventh victory under her belt, it was Ruffian's turn to attempt the "Triple Tiara," as the New York Racing Association chose to call it. It was in 1961 that NYRA decided to group three races together and call it the Filly Triple Crown. The first in the series would be the Acorn Stakes on May 10th at Aqueduct. Of the seven fillies in the race no one posed a serious challenge, but each got a look at the "new" Ruffian. While maintaining a serious presence, Ruffian did not charge to a runaway lead. Jacinto Vasquez had the filly respond to his efforts to keep her speed in check. This was the strategy and practice that would be needed for the longer races, which were yet to come.

While Ruffian was tromping her opponents in the Acorn, something very serious was happening at the betting windows. The betting on her was so significant that it had created a "minus pool." When this happens, the betting favors one horse to such a degree that there is not enough money to pay off all of the winning tickets, and the track must make up the difference. Any racetrack operator will avoid this at all cost, and sometimes place bets himself if a minus pool seems likely. When Ruffian ran in the Acorn the minus pool was over $30,000. This was the price that NYRA would have to pay for showcasing a star like Ruffian.

The Mother Goose Stakes would be a different kind of race for the filly. At a mile and an eighth, it would the first time that she would be asked to go more than one mile. Also, the track configuration at Aqueduct would demand two turns; some horses handle two turns well but no trainer can predict what a horse will do. Whiteley felt confident, and trusted Ruffian to take the turns in stride.

Within the first few seconds of the race, one horse, Dan's Commander, stumbled and fell, causing her rider to be thrown over her head. She was in the post-position next to Ruffian, but fortunately the filly was ahead at this point, and wasn't affected by the spill. While Ruffian took the turn a little wider than planned, she compensated and pulled ahead with a half-mile remaining. As she pulled away, she left the competition far behind and crossed the finish line thirteen and a half lengths ahead of the next contender. In her efforts Ruffian set a new record for the stakes, and was one step closer to her crown.

The Coaching Club American Oaks, at Belmont Park, would be the longest race to be run by the filly, at a mile and a half. For Ruffian, who gave her all from the starting gate to the finish line, this race would require patience with Vasquez guiding her effort. Among the field of seven, Equal Change may have been the only real competition. Ruffian drew away in the stretch in her usual style and crossed the finish line at two and three-quarter lengths ahead of the next filly. In the contest, she was not really pushed, but her time was two-fifths of a second better than Avatar, the colt that had won the Belmont Stakes two weeks before.

Although not as prestigious as the traditional Triple Crown, the Filly Triple Crown was still quite an accomplishment. The longstanding history associated with the Kentucky Derby distinguished it as the "greatest two minutes in sports." The fillies attempting the NYRA version had an equal challenge, but the media never booked it as such. In other years, a few fillies had taken the crown, including Dark Mirage (1968), Shuvee (1969) and Chris Evert (1974), but it was growing in popularity. With Ruffian's blend of speed and class, the events in 1975 got a lot of attention. Ruffian had become a real "media darling," even if her trainer did not want her to be.

An Imperfect Match

With her decisive capturing of the Filly Triple Crown, it was evident to all that Ruffian had clearly run out of female competition. Her injury in the fall of 1974 had sidelined Ruffian from her taking on the boys in the Champagne Stakes. All who knew Whiteley well realized that the Kentucky Derby, with all of its hype and press, would never be on his list, if it could have been avoided. At this point it looked as though a match of some sort was inevitable. It was one of the few years that there had been three individual winners for the colts' Triple Crown races, with no one repeating. The question now was, "Should she take on all three winners of the colts' Triple Crown races?"

Over in New Jersey, at Monmouth Park, there had been talk about a race pitting Ruffian against Foolish Pleasure, Master Derby and Avatar, the three colts who had won the Kentucky Derby, Preakness Stakes and Belmont Stakes respectively. On another front, New York Racing Association Chairman, Jack J. Dreyfus, Jr. was pushing to have New York sponsor the event, which would have tremendous fan appeal. As the details were being worked out, the Belmont Stakes winner, Avatar, left for California to prepare for the Swaps Stakes. The appeal of a race with only two instead of all three colts seemed to be limited, but there needed to be some sort of contest with Ruffian. In the *Blood-Horse*, Kent Hollingsworth had written, "Until these colts are measured against Ruffian, none of them has much claim to a title of Three Year Old Champion. Right now we do not believe that... any of them could catch up with Stuart Janneys' big filly."

Since the Coaching Club American Oaks was scheduled for the 21st of June, there were no possibilities on the calendar until July. Together, NYRA Chairman Dreyfus and Racing Secretary Noe set a date for the 6th of July. The race would carry a purse of $400,000: $225,000 for first place, $125,000 for second place and $50,000 for third place. Mrs. Robert Lehmann, owner of Preakness Stakes' winner, Master Derby, graciously accepted the invitation, as did the Janneys. If Whiteley had his way, there would have been no such contest, but the Janneys felt that the pressure was too great, and their options were limited. There was, however, strong opposition from the Foolish Pleasure contingent. His trainer, LeRoy Jolley, believed that Ruffian and Foolish Pleasure would dominate the race from the start, wear themselves out and hand the victory to Master Derby. After much discussion the problem was solved, but in a convoluted and questionable way. Mrs. Lehmann would be given the third place prize money, $50,000 if she would not participate. Reluctantly she agreed, and the Match Race was set with only two competitors, Ruffian and Foolish Pleasure.

When the match was officially on the calendar, the media took off like a house on fire. There was so much hype, that CBS, who had established the purse, chose to televise it nationally to some 20,000,000 viewers. If Whiteley thought that the Kentucky Derby was the only large-scale media circus, he wasn't prepared for the fever pitch of the up-and-coming weeks. This contest would not only attract a racing crowd, but a celebrity-seeking crowd and most of America as well.

Two years before the Great Match Race, as it was called, the feminist movement had come into its own with the defeat of tennis star Bobby Riggs at the hands of Billy Jean King. Proponents of the movement relished another opportunity to pit boy versus girl, and Ruffian had become their newest "poster child."

As the match gathered more and more momentum, people chose up sides. Buttons were made and distributed. Tee shirts reminiscent of the Ben Casey Show, displaying the male and female symbols, were hawked. For the first time, track betting would be permitted on a Sunday and the crowds would be out in full force.

The "match race" in horseracing was far from being a new concept; there had been many great matches over the years. In 1937, a post-depression crowd had listened to Triple Crown winner War Admiral take on Seabiscuit at the Great Pimlico Special. A number of years later, Nashua ridden by Eddie Arcaro would duel with Swaps ridden by Willie Shoemaker. The format had a way of capturing the public's attention, like two prizefighters going at it.

For Whiteley, it was all about money and he didn't have a choice. No trainer wants to see one of his best horses ridden out. In past matches, the leader from the beginning had always been the winner at the end. That was the only strategy. It was all out running and pressure from the gate on, for the entire mile and a quarter, with no let up. Ruffian had never been headed; she had also never run at her fastest speed. Whiteley had not allowed it. That had not been necessary for her to win a race, and Ruffian didn't need that kind of pressure.

The public began to compare numbers and races. Ruffian had won all of her 10 races and the Filly Triple Crown. The colt Foolish Pleasure had captured 11 out of 13 races, one of which was the Kentucky Derby. Ruffian was an exceptionally large filly at 16.2 hands, weighing 1125 pounds and wearing a size 5 shoe. On the other hand, Foolish Pleasure stood 15.3 hands, weighed 1061 pounds and wore a size 6.2 shoe. This last piece of information is important, for a horse lives and dies on its feet.

Vasquez had been aboard Ruffian for eight of her victories, but he was also Foolish Pleasure's regular rider. When it came to who would ride Ruffian, the jockey was given his choice.. Without hesitation and outside pressure, he chose Ruffian, "I liked the filly, she had a lot of potential to beat everyone around and that is why I chose the filly." The only lingering thought that seemed to bother Vasquez going forward was that LeRoy Jolley (Foolish Pleasure's trainer) would no longer use him as a regular ride, although it had never been said. To replace Vasquez, Jolley chose Braulio Baeza, who was an experienced jockey at coaxing extra speed from his horses.

Public sentiment was running high for the cause of the filly whom the bettors were sending off at the 2-5 odds-on favorite. Foolish Pleasure was set at 4-5.

On the day of the match, tents had been set-up on the grounds, and strains of the Preservation Hall Jazz Band could be heard everywhere. The atmosphere was electric. It was like the Super Bowl, the Stanley Cup and the World Series all put together. It was the most publicized race in the history of horseracing, as America waited for the very simple answer, "Who would win the Great Match Race?"

Throughout the entire time, Whiteley had been very protective of Ruffian. Even Stuart Janney, Jr. had said on the phone to Whiteley several times, if there were any reason for the filly not to run, we would call it off. Years later, Stuart Janney, III remembered his feelings, "We were very nervous, feeling like the weight of the world was on us."

As it neared six o'clock, dark storm clouds had formed everywhere. The sky was very, very dark, almost eerie, and there was a sense of foreboding. Whiteley waited until the last possible moment to bring Ruffian out. She wore a saddle-cloth with number 1 in the red and white silks of Locust Hill Farm. Being led by a pony, Foolish Pleasure followed with his number 2. The entire grouping with a red-coated outrider paraded in front of the grandstand. As they approached the starting gate, a record crowd at Belmont Park of 50,764 watched from the edges of their seats.

Both horses entered the starting gates without any difficulty. They would be occupying positions 2 and 3, with no one starting on the rail. When the starter George Cassidy saw that they were settled, he pressed the button springing the huge starting gates. Ruffian seemed to be startled and lunged forward striking her right ankle on the gate. Vasquez struggled to right himself, as both he and Ruffian leaned into Foolish Pleasure. Gathering herself Ruffian dropped back for a split second, and then charged to the lead. Both ran a smooth first quarter mile with Ruffian slightly ahead. Vasquez knew that the pace could not continue this way for another mile, and he settled Ruffian into her fast, fluid and effort-less motion.

In the second quarter mile, Ruffian seemed to be gaining an edge. As they neared the three-quarters pole, both jockeys heard a snap, as if a twig were breaking. Ruffian was leaning on her left side as her right leg collapsed beneath her. The jockey's response was immediate, as he began to pull her up with all of his strength. She kept going; she would not stop, as she moved another fifty yards on three legs. Her heart and spirit were pulling her on. Her desire to win was carrying her. In the background, the track announcer kept screaming, "Ruffian has broken down! Ruffian has broken down!" The crowd of 50,000 plus went silent, and Foolish Pleasure grew farther and farther away. He continued ahead as the stunned crowd watched. Foolish Pleasure was required to finish the race before others were permitted onto the surface. The race seemed to never end.

Desperate Measures

Ruffian was running on the stump of her right leg, with her hoof dangling by a few loose tendons. As she charged forward, the dirt mingled with the blood and bone fragments. Her sesamoids had exploded within her leg, and Vasquez was fighting the fight of his life to get her to stop. Finally Ruffian slowed, and Vasquez, with tears streaming down his face, jumped down to support her. An ambulance had been called, but no one could approach Ruffian until Foolish Pleasure had finished the race.

The first veterinarian to reach Ruffian was Manuel Gilman, the NYRA track veterinarian. His first thought was to apply an inflatable cast to her right leg with the hope of providing some support and stabilizing the shattered limb. In the process, both he and Ruffian were covered with her blood. Within seconds the ambulance arrived, and so did Frank Whiteley, his son David and Dr. Alex Harthill, who had treated Ruffian for her hairline fracture. In a group effort, they loaded the panicked and frightened horse into the ambulance to return her to her stall.

As a rule, horses are most comfortable in their own stalls. Few would say that Ruffian even knew where she was, as she struggled in agony on her three good legs. Those closest to her, Whiteley, Dan, Yates, Squeaky, Mike, David Whiteley and the vets, maneuvered in a frantic way to make her settle down. They submerged her shattered limb in ice water to try to control the excessive bleeding. This effort would serve as a further contaminant to the open wound, but at this point things could hardly get worse than they already were. Dr. Prendergast, a track vet, prepared an injection to calm the frantic horse, but the instability of her condition warranted giving small doses at a time. There were many drugs that Ruffian needed, but her system was so keyed up— her respiration and circulation were in over-drive—for her to receive them safely.

Outside, the media, employees and the Janneys were gathering. There was too much activity and it was bordering on bedlam. The size of the stall seemed to shrink before their eyes as Dr. Prendergast tried to bring in the portable x-ray machine. Everyone knew that Ruffian's sesamoids were shattered, but they needed pictures to drive the decisions that would be made. Just how crucial was surgery at this time? Could it wait until tomorrow when the filly was stabilized? She was in shock and had lost so much fluid. All systems were accelerated, and this only increased the risks involved with anesthesia. If they waited, would she accept some sort of cast or fixator on her leg until tomorrow? In the past she had only tolerated the equivalent of an ace bandage. This could not be the case with the extent of her injuries. Even sedation over night would have to be tempered to adjust to her fragile condition.

The decision was made to operate as soon as possible, as her condition was worsening. Past experience had shown that the filly would not respond to restraints of any kind. Ruffian had always been the boss and to think otherwise was to deny her very nature. She was high-strung, strong-willed and powerful. Docile and compliant were not in her vocabulary, and everyone who loved her knew it. If Ruffian were left in the stall any longer, she would destroy herself. She was a smart animal, and she knew that she was helpless. This is a terrible reality for any animal, let alone one whose 1125 pounds can no longer be supported by only three legs.

The ambulance transported a helpless Ruffian to Dr. William Reed's Equine Clinic, which was located across the street. As the filly was being loaded into the vehicle, Mr. and Mrs. Janney, feeling anxious, hovered nearby. Mr. Janney approached Dr. Harthill and inquired about the filly's chances for survival. The sad answer was returned, "Less than 10%." Both Janneys were distraught, but encouraged the team of veterinarians. "Please do all that is possible to try and save her." With those parting words, the owners turned and left.

It was a task to stabilize Ruffian in surgery. She would go so far under anesthesia that the doctors would need to apply stimulants. Then the stimulants would start to take over, and the anesthesia would need to be increased. It was truly a roller-coaster experience. Twice during the surgery the filly's heart stopped altogether, and she was revived. As the operation progressed, the greatest effort was needed to clean the dirt, gravel and grit from the injury site. If the filly had stopped running after the injury, the prognosis would have been a lot better. As the vets tried to piece together what resembled a bag of ice, they were attempting what probably would never have been considered for another horse. But Ruffian was special; she had won America's heart, and they had to try and work a miracle for the millions who were rooting for her. Most of her fans went to bed that night with the knowledge that her future was in good hands. Everything was being done to repair her broken leg.

Among the doctors present was an Edward O'Keefe. He was an orthopedic surgeon who was friendly with the Janney's niece, Cynthia Phipps. Although he was exclusively an orthopedist for human injuries, he had fashioned braces for horses in the past. There was a brace that he had made for a filly that wore the same size shoe as Ruffian. He offered to drive to his Long Island home to retrieve it for the injured filly. The vets were apprehensive, since Ruffian had been under anesthesia for some time, but they had few other options. When the brace was attached it required a casing of plaster of Paris. The total appliance weighed in excess of forty pounds.

Meanwhile, the outpouring of sympathy on the part of the public was overwhelming. People phoned and offered to send their vet, their private plane and donations galore. Calls were received from all over the United States, Canada and overseas. "Please save the filly! How can we help? What can I do? Tell me what it will cost. Whatever you need, we will help. Please try to save her."

As the operation continued so did the media intrusion. People were walking in and out of the hospital; it had become a regular Grand Central Station. Mr. Janney had returned after escorting his wife home, while Frank Whiteley and his staff anxiously waited for any news. As the filly was brought to the recovery room, all of her friends watched as she lay still. The room was encased in padding with a thick bed of straw on the floor. For Ruffian to survive, it would be necessary for her to awaken and stand on her feet. Horses cannot remain on their sides for any period of time, as the radial nerves in their shoulders can become paralyzed. As she would regain consciousness from anesthesia, everyone would await her reaction. It is natural for horses to flee from danger; instincts dictate that they run away.

When Ruffian awakened from the anesthesia, she began to run fast and furiously. She was finishing the race of her life; she was overtaking Foolish Pleasure at the turn; the finish line was in her sights. She ran, and ran, and ran. No one could hold her back. Each of the men had positioned himself on a leg or a side. Her strength was so overpowering that they were thrown around the room like rag dolls. Her cast had begun to slip. Her legs were crashing into each other. She became more violent and thrashed around the room. It was a flailing motion with her legs that no one could control. Even in her weakened state, she was a very powerful animal, whose instincts were out of control. The leg which had been broken was further damaged and bleeding. Other limbs were injured as well. It was out of the question to sedate her again, and any dose of tranquilizer could prove fatal. The men had run out of options.

Everyone had tried to reverse the odds. America had fallen in love with her and did not want to let her go. Then, there comes a point in the equation where continued attempts were prolonging her agony. She had reopened her original wounds and added new injuries to the old. Her dehydrated state was coupled with shock and pain that were greater than before the surgery. There was nowhere to go. The doctors knew it, the stable hands knew it and Whiteley knew it. The battle was over.

After conferring with the vets, Whiteley called Mr. Janney, to explain the developments. Mr. Janney's response was brief, "Please don't let her suffer anymore." Ruffian was given a fatal dose of anesthesia at 2:20 am on July 7, 1975, and was dead within 5 seconds.

Later that morning all of Whiteley's staff reported to the barn, just as they normally would, but things were anything but normal. For the first time Frank Whiteley admitted to his wife that he didn't want to go to the barn. There was no reason to go with Ruffian gone. He hid all of his emotions so well, but one can only take so much. The eight-hour ordeal had seemed like an eternity. The match race was supposed to provide the answer to one simple question, "Who was better?" Now, there were no answers. She was gone and America had lost its star because of a lot of money and a hyped-up race. Was it worth it? Most people would give a very simple answer, "No."

But Whiteley did go to the barn. No one said much because no one could. The entire racing world was in shock; it had taken a "punch to the gut." Many of the people who watched that race, had never watched a horse race before, and wouldn't watch one again. The whole experience was tinged with her blood, and people would not forget for a very long time, if ever. Later Frank Deford of *Sports Illustrated* would say, "She was the Titanic going down." She seemed invincible and immortal. When she breathed her last, she was in the lead. For the briefest of moments, her star was shining brighter than any other's, and now it was gone.

Ruffian's body would be buried that evening. The newly opened Kentucky Horse Park had offered space but Whiteley had another idea. The NYRA had hoped that she would be buried at Belmont Park. It was the scene of her first race and it was the scene of her last. There she would be in the middle of the infield of the park, which would forever claim her as its own. She belonged here and everyone knew it. She was their star and for the briefest of moments, she gave them a glimpse of perfection. As her large body, in a full white shroud, was lowered into its final resting place, she was to be facing the finish line and the Winner's Circle-the places that she knew so well. She was covered with her red and white Locust Hill Farm blankets at Whiteley's request. A single red rose was placed next to her, and the grave was closed forever.

Claiborne Farm enjoys a rich history of breeding many fine Thoroughbred race horses. Sire of the year (eight times) Bold Ruler (shown here twice) counted among his famous offspring the great Secretariat and Reviewer (Ruffian's sire). Shown is the foaling barn (the place of Ruffian's birth), the original racetrack and Ruffian's trainer, Frank Y. Whiteley, Jr.

CLAIBORNE FARM

Ruffian won all ten of her completed races. Among her greatest victories were the three jewels of the Filly Triple Crown: the Acorn Stakes (right), the Mother Goose Stakes (top left) and the Coaching Club American Oaks (top right).

The caricatures of Ruffian and Foolish Pleasure by Pierre E. Bellocq suggest the level of media participation. Ruffian's (top) comment to Foolish Pleasure – "I'll be with you in a minute."

The Great Match Race of July 6, 1975, was a media-driven competition between Filly Triple Crown-winning Ruffian and Kentucky Derby-winner Foolish Pleasure. As the race evolved into a "boy vs. girl" meeting, spectators found themselves choosing sides. Ruffian is shown posing the day before the race with groom Dan Williams and in Frank Whiteley's barn.

Ruffian was humanely euthanized at 2:20 am, July 7, 1975, eight hours after her breakdown during the Great Match Race. She was the first horse to be buried in the infield at Belmont Park with her nose facing the finish line and winner's circle. These were places that she knew well.

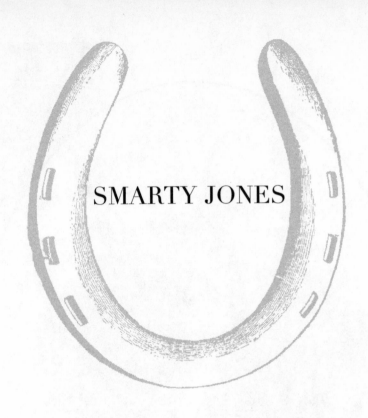

SMARTY JONES

"There was nothing about him that wasn't great." - Steve Haskin

Horse Racing in Pennsylvania

The rolling hills of southeastern Pennsylvania beckon from all directions to the serious-minded historian. More events impacting our nation's origins happened here, than in any other state. As the time-honored pages are turned, ghosts of times past give tribute to long-forgotten wars, political revolutions and historical milestones. Those stages were none other than the "Penn's Woods," of the Commonwealth's most famous son, William Penn. As Penn and early Quaker settlers made their mark on the nation's birth certificate, so, too, did their descendents impact all aspects of the life and culture of future Pennsylvanians.

In Colonial America, the earliest settlers came to this land seeking religious freedom. In Pennsylvania, the land lent itself to agriculture, and these colonists fared well laboring in something that was both familiar and sustaining. Their needs were few, their spirits strong and their lifestyle austere. For transportation they depended on their horses, but this engagement was one of need rather than sport. Horses were kept mainly as work animals, but on occasions were raced on familiar venues. Early documents suggest that they raced their horses as a means of determining the animal's quality, strength and value, but no financial remuneration was attached to the assessment.

During 1682, Pennsylvania's first Great Law was published, and it did not forbid the racing of horses as one might have expected. Traditional religious groups and stalwart Quakers frowned on the betting which accompanied the racing, but took few formal steps to stop it. Early chronicles suggest that William Penn even raced his English thoroughbreds on Philadelphia streets. One street in particular was used for this amusement and later became known as Race Street. Early plans of the city list a Sassafras Street among the other tree-named thoroughfares, and a visitor standing at the corner of Second and Race Streets may observe the name Sassafras chiseled into the side of an eighteenth century building on the corner.

Over time, horse racing became more of a public sport across the state. By the 1780s, Pittsburgh had a three-day event on the plain below Grant's Hill at the conclusion of the harvest. These races became social experiences and were very well attended by all family members. As the crowds grew larger these carnival-like celebrations, akin to state fairs, were compelled to relocate outside the city limits. In some instances, purses of substantial value were offered in the more organized stakes races, and this feature only helped to swell the crowds.

By 1794, Pennsylvania adopted its historic "Blue Laws," which banned "vain and frivolous amusement," as well as any gambling. A specific clause addressed horse racing "for any plate, prize, wager, bet, sum of money or other valuable thing." Within the next 10 years, other laws were created to further discourage the practice of racing. One such law forbad more than 15 people being assembled for the display, in an effort to dispel the crowds which had become unruly. Another declared racing to be a public nuisance and relegated the activity to public roads outside of the city and county limits. Regardless of the restrictions, more spontaneous racing events were taking place. Across the Commonwealth, other Race Streets were cropping up, as people relished the enjoyable and inexpensive entertainment that the races provided.

By 1820 it became apparent to all that the enforcement of the "Blue Laws" was basically non-existent. In areas removed from Quaker leaders or Presbyterian ministers, there was little or no compliance. These circumstances prompted the legislature to create a statewide ban on any horse racing. The document entitled, "An Act Against Horse Racing," leveled very high fines on any person found guilty of racing for purses or prizes. In more serious cases, a person's horse might even be confiscated. For moralists seeking strict enforcement of the law, a statewide tone had been set, which racing enthusiasts would battle for the next one hundred fifty years.

Being a largely rural state, agriculture held a key position among the workforce and within the state's economy. Many horsemen felt compelled to petition the state for speed trials to evaluate the work horses and to improve the breed. Proponents of the anti-racing law would challenge these requests as false pretenses for the continuation of the gambling, which accompanied the trials. The discussion became a "political football" of sorts and found its way to the agricultural fairs, where it came disguised in a different venue. Horses were trotted for the public as featured events, instead of the plowing matches of previous years. In 1856, the U.S. Agricultural Society Fair was held in West Philadelphia, and over 50,000 people turned out to watch the speed trials. Trotting was received equally as well by the fans, and soon found its place at all local and county fairs. This trend seemed to slide by the conservatives without too much ill will, until some felt that the livestock exhibitions and educational aspects of the fair were being ignored. As was noted in *The Public Ledger (Philadelphia)*, "There is danger that agricultural fairs may be ruined by transforming them into race courses."

With the advent of the trotters came a "trade-off" with the conservative faction. Many of the more conspicuous purse races had been discontinued, but the average citizen was still taking great delight in watching and racing horses. Most of the trotters were standardbreds, a hardy American hybrid of the thoroughbred and other riding strains, and could be used for pulling carts or driving freight, an issue of high appeal for most in the agricultural community.

As the community-at-large welcomed the trotters, space and tracks became areas of immediate concern as the need for smooth and unencumbered surfaces became apparent. With the opening of Hunting Park in the 1820s, Philadelphia became the first city in the country to prepare and endorse a track for trotting. In compliance with the state law, races were held as matinees with no fees or cash awards. Many other cities within the Commonwealth followed suit, and opened "driving parks" for the improvement and the advancement of the working horse.

By 1879, the General Assembly of Pennsylvania amended the 1820 law, and voted to permit racing for prizes and purses at county fairs. This was the first formal admission by state lawmakers that the sport had universal appeal, especially in the more rural areas. This proclamation served as a further anointing of the trotters as part of the fabric of the most popular social institution—the county fair. The next 10 years would witness the advent of many new "driving parks" and tracks across the state of Pennsylvania.

In 1888, York and Reading opened new tracks with ample grandstands, and the Allentown Fair, in 1902, sported a newly-improved grandstand accommodating 2,200 people and complete with restaurant and dining facilities. The "City of Brotherly Love" joined its sister city, Pittsburgh, in constructing a large "driving park." In Pittsburgh, Homewood Park was already on the Grand Central Circuit, a nationally-organized group that featured the best trotters and the largest purses. With its construction in 1889, Philly's Point Breeze Park would become part of the circuit and join the "Golden Age of Trotting."

The rapid and fervent growth of the trotters in Pennsylvania now fueled the state's legitimate need for invigorating the horse-breeding industry. At the turn of the century, Hanover Shoe Company owners, Harper Sheppard and Clinton Myers, opened a modest stable with the intention of raising trotters for the newly-inaugurated state fair circuit. After twenty years, their efforts had paid off a hundredfold, as they were the proud owners of the largest breeding operation of standardbreds in the world. That is an accolade which rings true, even to today.

At the turn of the century in Pennsylvania, there was not one legitimate thoroughbred racing track in the entire state. Those who embraced racing in all its forms supported the trotters, but waited anxiously for a change of heart to accept the thoroughbreds on a state level. It didn't come. In New York in 1909, things seemed to be working in reverse. Governor Hughes was decrying the existence of commercial horse-racing tracks by calling them sources of graft and corruption. With these rumblings so close to home, Pennsylvania lawmakers continued to fend off efforts at reinitiating the on-going debate and held their ground. As the battle continued, harness racing at the county fairs continued to be well attended on all levels, and drew spectators from neighboring venues. Through the 1940s, Allentown and York continued to be prominent stops along the way, as they showcased the best in Pennsylvania born and bred horses.

Some of the wealthier Pennsylvanians were supporting thoroughbred racing efforts in other states. In 1918, at a Saratoga sale, Samuel Riddle paid $5,000 for one of August Belmont's colts. The colt returned to Glen Riddle Farm, and soon the world was introduced to the great Man O' War. Riddle was only one of many staunch supporters of thoroughbred racing from the Philadelphia area. The Wideners, George and his uncle, Joseph, were regular attendees at some of the most prestigious tracks, as well as owners of breeding and training operations within Pennsylvania. In New York, the Jockey Club was founded, and many of these Pennsylvanians held key positions, especially George Widener, who served as chairman for a number of years.

For the wealthy in the Philadelphia area, interest in racing was manifested in the local hunt clubs. There were clubs in Radnor, Rose Tree and Huntington Valley, that had annual race gatherings which featured fox hunts, steeple chases and "flat" racing. For many of the more-socially elite, these were highlights in the social calendar.

Once again in 1927, efforts were made to legalize pari-mutuel horse racing through a bill prepared by Charles Baldi, a Representative from Philadelphia. Optimism grew as this bill passed through committee, only to be shot down by the General Assembly. The vote was 119 to 50, and to many it seemed that little had changed in one hundred years.

As the Depression neared its end, many of the states neighboring Pennsylvania legalized thoroughbred horse racing. This trend brought additional pressure to local lawmakers, but most held fast to their positions. There appeared to be very little support among rural legislators.

On the harness-racing circuit, things were alive and well. In all areas of the state, Pennsylvanians flocked to local county fairs setting record numbers for attendance. Among the significant tracks were those in York and Allentown, which always packed a full house as they showcased local Pennsylvania-bred stars.

By the 1950s, several other standardbred breeding farms were operating within the state, in addition to the very successful Hanover Stable. These included: the Meadow Lands Farm, Lana Loebell Farm and the Hempt Farm. Their efforts collectively had produced some of the greatest harness racers in the world.

In September 1959, a bill to legalize pari-mutuel betting at licensed harness tracks in the state of Pennsylvania finally passed through the state House of Representatives by one vote. Four months later the bill was signed into law by Governor Lawrence, and citizens could finally shake off the shackles of almost a century and a half of conservative domination. The tracks would be overseen through the Department of Agriculture, and soon serious plans were in the works.

Within three years harness- racing tracks were up-and-running within the state. In June of 1963, the first harness races were held at Liberty Bell Park in Philadelphia and Meadows Racetrack in Washington County. Two years later Pocono Downs in Luzerne County would follow their lead. While this was encouraging to most racing fans, others yearned for the thoroughbred racing, which they so eagerly supported in other states.

Inspired by the success of the newly-created harness-racing tracks across the state, the General Assembly legalized "flat" thoroughbred racing tracks in 1967, and created a specific commission to monitor their efforts. Interested parties canvassed the state for suitable locations. In Philadelphia, the fledgling efforts of over 200 years were finally rewarded, when the first thoroughbreds ran at Liberty Bell Park in June, 1969. By 1974, three more new tracks had been added—Keystone Race Track in Bensalem Township, Bucks County (later to be called Philadelphia Park), Penn National in East Hanover Township, Dauphin County and Commodore Downs in Erie.

In the first thirty years of legalized racing, the citizens have embraced the industry by bringing some of the statistics to all time highs. Within the state itself there have been over 2,800 different operations involving over 26,000 horses. As Pennsylvania's agricultural community could attest, these breeding and training facilities utilized almost $20 million dollars in grain and feed supplements alone, which helped to support the statewide income. More jobs had been created through the tracks and farms, as Pennsylvania strove to become a competitive stop on the racing circuit.

Through all of this history, it has been an uphill climb. There have been wonderful thoroughbred horses born and bred in Pennsylvania that have gone on to do great things in the racing world. The prolific sires, Danzig, Lymphard and Storm Cat, have their origins here, as well as the wonderful filly, Go for Wand. In 1992, the Kentucky Derby winner, Lil E. Tee was born in the Keystone State, which meant a great deal to the people who lived there.

With the advent of the new millennium, few people would have believed what great things would be in store for the people of Pennsylvania. Patricia and Roy Chapman of Someday Farm in Chester County were two of those people. The Chapmans had enjoyed some modest success in their racing efforts since 1987, and were preparing for a new foal that would be coming along in 2001. At the time of the breeding, it was very important to them that the offspring of I'll Get Along would be Pennsylvania born and bred. Little did they know what the racing gods had in store for them.

Someday Farm

When one hears the name "Someday Farm," images are conjured up that are mystical, magical and even mysterious. Legends are created around places that sound like this, and any wordsmith could easily celebrate it as a wonderful place to be. For Pat and Roy Chapman, this farm represented all of their hopes, dreams and aspirations. When they purchased the farm it had been called Someday Farm. This sign was retired to the barn, as Pat and Chappy sought to come up with a new name and new sign that would speak to their racing interests, and capture their blue and white Chapman silks. In choosing this new name for the farm, they played with ideas for months. As Pat would later say, "We used to say 'someday' we're going to do this, and 'someday' we're going to do that. We should name this place Someday Farm." They did adopt the name, the once-removed sign was collected from the barn, but the legend would come later.

At their farm in Chester County, the Chapmans reveled in the beauty of one of the most stunning areas of horse farms in the state of Pennsylvania. To some of the more long-standing farms in the county, Walnut Green and Brushwood Stables to name a few, the Chapmans may have seemed like newcomers with only fourteen years under their belts. Prior to 2000, some of their successes had been notable. Their very first race horse Small Victories (in 1987) won its first race, and they were hooked. Two years later they would meet great success on the steeplechase circuit with Uncle Merlin, and a win in the Maryland Hunt Cup. Uncle Merlin would go on to compete in the English Grand National in 1990, and place third.

In the arena of thoroughbred racing, they had tested the waters at Philadelphia Park, but with limited success. Their trainer Bob Camac was a well-loved icon of sorts, whose knowledge and expertise had elevated him among his peers. As Chappy (Roy) would say, "He just loved horses…no better horseman in the business." These thoughts were echoed many times by those who knew and understood Bob's thoroughness, knowledge and his attention-to-detail. For these reasons and many more, the Chapmans entrusted all of their horses to Bob Camac.

For those who know anything about training horses, Bob Camac was a journeyman trainer, coming up through the ranks, and he knew his business. He knew how to put "bottom" on a horse, and he knew winning combinations when he saw them. Having established his bases at Philadelphia and Delaware Parks, Bob Camac was well respected among his clients. He encouraged the Chapmans to acquire a yearling from the Keeneland sale. This previously unnamed filly would soon become I'll Get Along, and she became a formidable presence on the racetrack. With stakes wins in her pedigree, I'll Get Along would go on to become a desirable broodmare and a very worthwhile business investment. When it came time for her to be bred, Bob Camac researched his options well. After consulting many pedigrees, he chose a desirable sire, and approached the Chapmans with his plan.

In choosing a sire for I'll Get Along, Bob Camac selected Elusive Quality, who at the time was considered a young and relatively-untested sire. On the track, he had set some significant records on both turf and dirt, and as esteemed bloodstock agent Russell B. Jones has noted, "He was a seriously fast horse…and this was not a fluke of a pedigree. It was a very strong pedigree." The sire of Elusive Quality was Gone West, whose sire had been the great Mr. Prospector. As a sire, Gone West had historically thrown a lot of speed to his offspring, and Camac was looking for both speed and stamina. On the dam side, I'll Get Along, and her dam had both been stakes winners, and would bring a lot of potential to the union. On both sides of the pedigree there were tie-ins to Triple Crown winners of the past, with Secretariat being on the sire side and Seattle Slew on the dam side. In all aspects of his planning, Camac had surely done his homework, and the Chapmans were thrilled with the prospects of this union.

The dam I'll Get Along would travel to Kentucky for the breeding, but immediately return to Pennsylvania. The Chapmans would bring her back to their Someday Farm, and the foaling would take place there. The new foal would be Pennsylvania-born, and that was something that was important to both Pat and Chappy. What the Chapmans had no way of knowing, short of a crystal ball, was that the breeding community in Kentucky in 2000 would be struck with a horrid illness, and lose over 500 foals. The disease, which became known as Mare Reproductive Loss Syndrome or MRLS, was believed to be carried by caterpillars. The caterpillars would feast on leaves from the black cherry trees, and these leaves contained cyanide. Many of the mares ingested the caterpillars, hence poisoning their unborn foals. The end result was that hundreds of these foals in Kentucky were stillborn. Of the 55 mares that were bred that year to Elusive Quality, sixteen foals were stillborn, and all of these were in Kentucky.

Back in Chester County, I'll Get Along spent her entire time with the Chapmans. On the evening of February 28th, 2001, she was assisted in her delivery by the very capable farm manager, Deb Given. Bringing lots of experience to the task, Deb took a hold of the front feet and gave a good tug. The new mother wasn't known as Mrs. Congeniality to those at Someday Farm, and Deb had taken a few good kicks from her in her day. All involved were anxious that many of her good points be passed on to the new foal, and leave the disposition gene behind. All things considered, it was an uneventful foaling, and mother and baby colt did well.

The date of February 28th was a special day for Pat Chapman, as it had been her deceased mother Mildred's birthday. She pondered ways that the young colt could be named for her mother, but both she and Chappy knew that Mildred was totally out of the question. Early records show that he was registered as Get Along, a derivative of his dam's name. After some thought, Pat decided to call him Smarty Jones, a nickname that was frequently used by Mildred's grandfather, Papa Jones. At times Pat's mother may have acted precociously or been somewhat of a smart aleck, hence she received the name. The name seemed to fit the young foal's disposition as a bit of a trickster, so Pat paid the $100 to make it an official "Smarty Jones."

Over the next few months, Smarty and his mom spent all of their time together at the farm. Those who oversaw their care noticed Smarty's early precocious ways. He was a smaller foal with a take-charge attitude. His body was well-proportioned and gave evidence of real athleticism. As Bob Camac and the Chapmans watched him grow and develop, it was with genuine curiosity. Everyone wondered if he would become all that the most positive aspects of his pedigree suggested. If it all came together, he could be great. What was needed, was the time to wait and see.

As the fall of 2001 came around, Camac discussed shipping the yearling to George Isaacs at Bridlewood Farm in Ocala. As a trainer of yearlings and an assessor of talent, Isaacs's reputation had preceded him. He was the general manager of the farm, and had been in the business for over thirty years. Many champions had passed through his hands, including the all-time money winner, Cigar. Over the years, Isaacs had broken many yearlings, and turned them into top-notch race horses. He had worked well for the Chapmans in the past, and he was a dear and close friend of Bob Camac. Both Pat and Chappy concurred with Camac that a phone call needed to be made to George Isaacs to set things up before the first of the year. Unfortunately, Bob Camac never made that call, for he and his wife Maryann were found brutally murdered on December 6, 2001 at their New Jersey home.

The murder of Bob Camac, by his stepson Wayne Matthew Russell over a financial dispute, had a horrific effect on the Chapmans and the entire racing community. As Pat recalled, "We were devastated on many levels. Not only did we lose a good friend and an honest horse trainer, but we lost someone who made decisions for us, who made all of that easy for us." He was their trainer and friend, but he was also little Smarty's godfather of sorts. All of the plans for this colt had been so carefully detailed; with him gone, the Chapmans found them-selves at a veritable crossroad. Pat remembered, "We relied on Bob for a lot of things. We just didn't know if we had it in us to go through another trainer at that time." The Chapmans had been downsizing their operations, as Chappy's emphysema was taking its toll and his lifestyle had become more limited. Was it time to pack it all up and quit, or try to rebuild and move on? It was a very diffi-cult decision, but in the end the Chapmans did both. Many of their horses were sold, the farm was closed and they moved to Bucks County. A band of seven or eight adult horses were to be kept at Philadelphia Park, and only two yearlings remained — Some Image and Smarty Jones. To this day, Pat Chapman will tell you that she kept Smarty because "He had that look in his eye." With that said, it was time for the Chapman Boys to go to racing school.

On January 2, 2002, the two yearlings arrived at George Isaacs's in Ocala. At the time the Chapmans were devastated, but the idea of selling the two boys had never become an option. Part of them wanted to see the legacy of Bob Camac live on in the horse bearing Pat's mother's nickname, but another side was so wracked with grief that they were turning a page. Immediately, Isaacs was impressed with Smarty's speed and promise. Both boys stayed and learned the ropes, but Isaacs had already seen something in Smarty that he liked very much. The issue of selling Smarty never really amounted to much. When Isaacs told Chappy about the colt's gameness, he responded, "Since you like him so much, we'll try him."

By the spring of 2003, Smarty was ready to try the track. Isaacs took him to the training track to work a quarter mile, looked at his watch and smiled to himself. The next phone call was made to Pennsylvania, and the message to Chappy was simple, "He went 23, and made it look easy…I think this is the horse you've been waiting for your whole life." When it was time for the Chapman Boys to ship north, Isaacs took Smarty's shoes and hung them in his office. For a while he would keep the secret to himself; these shoes were going to be worth something someday, and someday was going to be sooner than he thought.

Team Smarty

When Pat and Chappy received George Isaacs's assessment of Smarty, they were genuinely pleased, but there was another large challenge looming. What were they going to do for a trainer now that Bob was gone? Upon the advice of another trainer and bloodstock agent, Mark Reid, the Chapmans hired John Servis. In the '80s, Reid had worked with Pat and Chappy, knew their style and understood their situation. He felt that it would be a good match because of the commonalities which existed. Both Servis and the Chapmans operated out of Philadelphia Park and had done very well as minor league players. This new colt deserved a chance, and they came to a mutual understanding about trying things out.

Before too long John Servis received a call from George Isaacs, to prepare him for the wonderful superstar that was coming his way. Never having seen the horse, Servis was a bit cautious. When the van arrived and the horses were unloaded, the caution immediately turned to skepticism. As the entire Servis staff stood and watched, the most beautiful, large, powerful and handsome horse stepped off the ramp. Everyone was duly impressed, for the horse was stunning. Those goose bumps were short- lived, when they heard the horse's name—Some Image. As the other horse exited the van, John Servis took a deep breath and mentally examined his options. "How do I get myself out of this contract, before I've gotten in too far?" The horse was small, and not at all what he expected. Before too much time had passed, Servis was back on the phone to George Isaacs, to address whether this whole thing was a joke. Isaacs's only words were, "Call me after he gets to the track." A few days later Smarty took his first workout; there were no more phone calls to Florida.

From his earliest days, Smarty had suggestions of greatness written all over him. He had the potential, the ability and the heart to make good things happen. All of those who had ever cared for him, saw something very special there. It was going to take a little bit more time, the right environment and the right people to make it happen. Chasing this very real and wonderful dream, was the beginning of "Team Smarty."

Against the enormous backdrop of thoroughbred racing, the Chapmans may have been considered small time players. They had entered the racing end of it somewhat later in life, but enjoyed every minute of it. You would never see them lining up at the large sales several times a year, where millions are dropped in a minute. It wasn't about the money; rather it was about how they chose to spend it, in a sport that they genuinely enjoyed.

For Pat Chapman, her earliest roots were in the southern tradition of the fine state of Georgia. Later in her life, the family moved to New Jersey. In addition to the full time job of being a divorced mother of two, a son and a daughter, Pat had chosen a career in social work. After her undergraduate degree, she completed a Masters in Social Work from Bryn Mawr College. She first became acquainted with Roy Chapman, when she went shopping for a new car. As the fates would have it, she acquired a lovely new Ford Granada. Sometime later, Chappy was fortunate to get a date with Pat, and a wonderful relationship was born.

On the other hand, Roy "Chappy" Chapman was a Philadelphia boy through and through, and he was very proud of that fact. He had been raised in Germantown, and had come from humble beginnings. As Chappy would tell you himself, "I was not born on a horse farm. I was born on the streets of Philadelphia. My grandfather rented horses out to pull ice wagons, produce carts and milk wagons. When they would bring them back, I would ride the ponies at night." In addition to working his way up in the horse world, so too, did Chappy come up from the grass roots in the auto industry. For years he had worked for John B. White, before acquiring the dealership himself. From this small beginning, he branched out to found Chapman Auto Group, which has a formidable presence in the Pennsylvania, New Jersey and Delaware area. Even in retirement, Chappy would keep his finger on the pulse, and would call his sons, Michael and Randy, if sales appeared to be down.

After their marriage in 1982, the Chapmans assumed a very active life style, of which horses were only a part. They sailed up and down the Eastern Seaboard and spent time deep-sea fishing. When home in Pennsylvania, the Chapmans enjoyed fox hunting at local venues, here and in Maryland. They were engaged in many, many things, until health issues became significant. Over the years, Chappy had developed emphysema, which had begun to take a toll on his activity level. Time was divided between Pennsylvania and Florida to avoid those harsh Pennsylvania winters. By the time Smarty Jones was coming into his own, Chappy had begun using oxygen throughout the day as well as adopting the power wheelchair as a further support. He would struggle with this disease, which was shackling his body but not his mind and his spirit. On days that were difficult, Smarty Jones would be his best medicine.

The Chapmans' beginning in the thoroughbred horse business occurred in 1987. Within a year, they purchased Someday Farm. At the peak of their involvement, they may have had 20 horses, which were raced mainly at Philadelphia Park. As Chappy would relate, "We learned how to do things, although not at a high level. We were ham-and-eggers, but we got to be players in our own league." Yes, they had become players, but in a league larger than they could have imagined. Smarty Jones was about to become a significant player on a national stage.

When the Chapmans approached John Servis, he had been training in the Philadelphia area for twenty years. Originally a native of Charlestown, West Virginia, Servis had spent his entire life with horses. His father Joe had devoted fifty years of his life to the industry, and had worked on every level. When John expressed an interest in a horse-related career, his father obtained a job for him that would help him make a good decision. John would remember, "When I was 14, I went to work in a barn. I think that my father told the owner to let me do everything except work with the horses. He wanted to be sure that I was committed." This experience proved to be worth its weight in gold. For Joe Servis, the only way you really understood horses was to work "from the ground up."

In examining his priorities, John Servis set his family first and his horses second. With wife Sherry, a high school sweetheart, and sons Tyler and Blane, Servis enjoyed all aspects of his family life and equine career. He could have moved up to the more prestigious New York circuit, but he probably wouldn't be genuinely happy. "I'd love to have a barnful of good horses," he said, "but I want to be happy, and my family to be happy, so it would have to be somewhere we would all enjoy being....I'm a country boy at heart." While still in West Virginia, John had tried his hand at Shepherdstown College, but it was not meant to be. Once involved with horses on a fulltime basis, he moved rapidly from grooming to agenting to training. Again, it was as Joe Servis said, "from the ground up."

With Smarty Jones arriving at the Servis Stable there were assessments to be made. All of this blistering speed would need to be harnessed properly and meaningfully directed. There were possible equipment changes to be considered, workouts to be adjusted and a jockey to be chosen. The last part was the easiest of all for John Servis, he would turn to his friend of many years, Stewart Elliott.

As a jockey Stewart Elliott was a journeyman, if there ever was one. The Elliott family had gone back through at least five generations of horsemen with their origins in Scotland. He had grown up within the industry in Canada with his father Dennis, a jockey- turned trainer, and his mother Myhill, an assistant trainer. He was born in Toronto, Canada, although a large part of his career had been spent within the United States. When he was sixteen, he quit school to become a jockey. His mother had hoped that he would be a veterinarian, but he heard another calling. As Stew explained, "The only thing I ever wanted to be was a jockey. I quit school at 16 to ride races. It's all I really know how to do." This dream was very real and he made it happen.

Things were going well until Stew was sidelined with a serious injury. A horse had thrown him, and he landed on the inner rail. While recuperating, he sat out for the duration but gained excessive weight. There was no place for that in the jockeys' room, as they slave daily to maintain unrealistic weights, which can compromise the body in many ways. Stew told his mother that he feared that he would never be able to lose the weight, and regain his position. For eighteen months he struggled with this terrible dilemma; he belonged on the track, but what else could he do? He recalls, "I thought about being a blacksmith or a horse dentist, but I went back to riding."

Over the years, Stewart had ridden over 20,000 races with more than 3,250 wins. In 1989 alone he had won 381 races, and had been the leading rider at Philadelphia Park for the previous three years. For Servis, he was a solid rider on whom John could place his trust. Stew had overcome a number of personal hurdles in the past, and was not above speaking about them to the media when asked. "I have nothing to hide. I've had a lot of personal problems and done some things that I'm not proud of. But that's behind me. I just want to look ahead to the future," related Elliott. Both Pat and Chappy, as recovered alcoholics for over thirty years each, reached out to Stewart Elliot and supported him throughout his troubles.

Together Team Smarty was about to embark on a once-in-a-lifetime journey that was beyond their wildest imaginings. Through it all, they would stick together with an incredible sense of loyalty. To date, things were shaping up like a soap opera. There had been a ruthless murder, an equine epidemic, serious health issues, a sold property, a trainer crisis, a challenged jockey and a feisty little horse, who wasn't finished with his part of the tail, or tale.

The Philly Flyer

It had been only twelve days since Smarty's arrival at John Servis's stable at Philadelphia Park. He had strutted his stuff, and sufficiently impressed most of the staff and trainers at the park. Some of the locals had taken to giving him some nicknames, which included the Philly Flash or the Philly Flyer, because of his brilliant and blazing speed. Ordinarily this wouldn't have meant anything, but it is thought that Smarty may have overheard these names and gotten delusions of grandeur. On July 28, 2003, the Philly Flyer made his first visit to a starting gate.

While at Bridlewood Farm in Ocala, Smarty had practiced with the starting gate. He had many successful sprinters in his pedigree. Sprinters can be so overly anxious to get out and run, that some are not comfortable with the gate. Milton Hendry from Bridlewood commented about Smarty's experience with starting gates, "He was never afraid of the gate, but he was always antsy inside. He would walk right in, but you just knew that he could blow up in there at any time." What Hendry predicted was only an understatement of what was destined to happen.

Assistant trainer Maureen Donnelly and exercise rider Peter Van Trump prepared Smarty by taking him to a practice starting gate, much like the kind he had experienced in Florida. Before Donnelly could enter the gate, Smarty reared up and lunged in an attempt to scale the large steel bar which topped the front of the starting gate. He struck his head with such incredible force that Donnelly and Van Trump thought he was dead. Within seconds he lay there unconscious in a pool of blood with his head tucked underneath his front legs.

One of the training assistants was able to revive the horse enough to get him out of the gate and to take inventory of his injuries. An initial assessment suggested that he had only bloodied his nose, and this would not be uncommon for a neophyte in a practice gate experience. After a closer inspection, things were progressively getting worse. Van Trump recalled, "His eye and whole head were already starting to swell up and there was blood coming out of everywhere." Even before he reached Servis's barn, a call had been placed to the emergency care unit.

The substituting veterinarian that day was Dr. Hanf who found Smarty to be in a great deal of pain. "He was profusely gushing blood out of both nostrils and his mouth as well," related Hanf. After many interventions they were unable to stop the bleeding. Finally, the horse was sedated in an attempt to lower the blood pressure. All of the wounds were cleaned several times and both antibiotics and anti-inflammatory drugs had been administered. When Dr. Hanf left Smarty at 4:00 pm he felt that the animal had been stabilized. The horse looked very ugly but appeared to be acting normally.

Upon Dr. Hanf's return at 6:00 am the following morning, Smarty had taken a turn for the worse. His head was grotesquely swollen, filled with large amounts of fluid and breathing issues could be detected. The horse's left eye was not visible at all and the noisy breathing suggested that the sinuses were seriously injured, too. Dr. Hanf wasted no time in directing John Servis to contact Dr. Patricia Hogan at the New Jersey Equine Center, and tell her that she would be receiving an emergency very soon. Dr. Hanf, Bill Foster and others at the barn detected a sense of foreboding as they watched Smarty Jones being prepared for transport. For the first time it was starting to look like the colt's life was in serious danger.

When Smarty had initially struck his head, John had phoned the Chapmans to apprise them of the accident. It was 7:00 am, and John began by saying, "Mr. Chapman , one of your horses has been injured." Chappy responded, "You don't even have to tell me which one; it's Smarty, isn't it? The slow ones never get hurt." Now another phone call was in order, to convey the gravity of the accident and Smarty's impending hospitalization.

When Smarty arrived at Dr. Hogan's, she was visibly surprised by what she saw. In his description of Smarty's injuries Dr. Hanf had not minimized anything, but Dr. Hogan was surprised by the horse's disposition. He entered the clinic with his ears up and acting very spunky, although his head was, "swollen to more than three times its normal size, bleeding from his left nostril and his eye swollen completely shut," she remembered.

Having given him a much more thorough examination, Dr. Hogan determined that Smarty would not lose his left eye, but had sustained multiple fractures to his skull. These included: his forehead, nasal bone, frontal sinus and eye socket. She had seen all of the injuries before but not all at the same time. He was given some pretty powerful antibiotics and anti-inflammatory drugs; his entire head was bandaged with the exception of his right eye and the tips of his ears. The staff nicknamed him Quasimodo, from the hunchback of Notre Dame, because of his grotesque appearance. But underneath the ugly injuries there lurked a heart of gold and soon Smarty had endeared himself to all on staff. No one could understand how a horse with all of these serious problems could be so pleasant. While hospitalized Smarty never missed a meal, greeted all guests upon their arrival and acted genuinely pleased to be there.

In two weeks, Smarty was discharged from the hospital. He was sent to Cedar Lane Farm for recuperation and rehabilitation. He would remain there for another six weeks. The questions still hanging in the balance were, "Would he ever be able to enter a starting gate again?" and if he did, "Would he be able to race?"

After his time at Cedar Lane it was time to return to Philadelphia Park. This was accompanied by loud cheering and clapping from the Barn 11 family, who doubted that they would ever see the colt again. Smarty Jones was back and he started to act like his old self again. Bill Foster recalled, "He wasn't back in that barn for five minutes before you knew what he was thinking. 'Come on, you guys, we got work to do'....There is not another horse in this world that could've come back from that." Well, he did make it to the track and acted as if nothing had happened. When Dr. Hogan heard the news, she was elated, "Smarty's head could have swelled to ten times its normal size, and it still wouldn't have been as big as his heart. He is a very special animal."

Now that it appeared that Smarty was almost back to his old self there was work to be done. If he were ready, some thought needed to be given to when and where his first race would be. In Ocala, George Isaacs was pulling for a New York debut. The horse would be seen by a more elite crowd and engage more media attention. In his heart Chappy had a fond feeling for the summer at Saratoga, but Smarty's injury had pushed his debut to the fall. The most important consideration surrounded what was best for Smarty coming off of his accident, and the Chapmans deferred the big decision to John Servis.

Considering all that the horse had been through, John had a much different perspective on the running of Smarty's first race. He didn't want to see the horse have to travel and he reminded the Chapmans and everyone else, that no one had any real idea what Smarty would do on the track. As a trainer, he was pushing for keeping it simple. He told the Chapmans that he'd pick a nice race at Philadelphia Park with some modest competition, and see what happens.

After reviewing the racing schedule, John chose November 9, 2003 as Smarty's first race. The horse had made trips to the starting gate since the accident, and after pausing for a few seconds seemed to put all the demons behind him and move on. This first race being at Philadelphia Park on a familiar track would hopefully reduce the amount of stress. As the race began Smarty moved like a pro under the direction of Stewart Elliott. After 6 furlongs in a time of 1:11 minutes, Smarty Jones had won his first race. All that could be heard at the park was Keith Jones the announcer's voice booming, "It's all Smarty Jones, and he wins by a staggering seven and a half lengths."

The colt proved to be more resilient than anyone would have expected. In two weeks, Servis announced that Smarty would run in the Pennsylvania Nursery Stakes at Philadelphia Park. Since all thoroughbreds receive January first as their official birthday, Smarty was nearing the end of his two-year-old season. Through circumstances beyond his control, he had not run nearly as many races as other two year old sensations, and even though his numbers may have been very good, he would not be considered for any two-year-old awards. This was hardly important to Team Smarty as they continued to prepare for the Nursery Stakes.

In Smarty's first race he had occupied postposition number nine. For the Nursery he would be running from postposition five, in a longer race than before, and against a stronger field. As the gate opened he stumbled and gave everyone a real scare. In seconds he righted himself, and took Stewart Elliott for another fantastic run ending with a victory margin of fifteen lengths. His time was 1:21 1/5 minutes and he set a blistering number for the Beyer Speed Index. In the Beyer, horses are assigned numbers based on their times during the race itself. Many predictions concerning aptitude and performance can be assessed using the Beyer.

It was time for John Servis to set sights outside of the Philadelphia area. If he wanted to find a place on the Derby trail, he needed to see what Smarty could do in a bigger, stronger field—like New York. During the winter months, all of the racing took place at Aqueduct, on Long Island. John chose to enter Smarty Jones in his first graded stakes race, the Count Fleet on January 3, 2004 at 1 mile plus 70 yards. There would be more depth to the field, he would be trying a longer race, and the race would be on a different track. All aspects of the test were in place and everything largely depended on what Smarty would do with it.

During the first two races, John Servis had seen an inordinate amount of speed from Smarty, but he did not see the horse settle in at any point in the races. As the races were increasing in length it was going to be fundamental for Stewart to get the horse to relax. Smarty would classically leave the gate (or stumble as he had in the first two races), catch up with the field and then blow past everyone to win. For future, longer races, some of this speed would have to be bottled, and then released as he came down the stretch. By going to the Count Fleet, John Servis could make a better decision based on how the horse would handle two turns and how well he could settle in.

By all assessments, Smarty Jones ran this race as he had run the others. He stumbled from the gate, caught the pack and charged across the finish line five lengths ahead of the competition. John did learn two significant things from the race: the horse could handle two turns but he could not relax. One out of two isn't bad, but John did have his work cut out for him.

The Road Through Arkansas

When John Servis made the decision to take Smarty Jones to Arkansas for his pre-Derby races, it was with a great deal of thought and planning. In an eight week period he had won three races but he had lost most of his two year old season due to a variety of issues. For all intent and purposes, Smarty was lucky to be alive, but in racing terms he was behind many of his contemporaries. Some had raced in the spring and summer, so there was some real catching up to do, and not much time to do it.

Traditionally, the good two-year olds are sent to Florida or California to some of the most premier tracks in the country. As the horses turn three on January 1, they participate in a series of races spanning January through April, that become somewhat of a selection process for the Kentucky Derby in early May. Many of these races are graded stakes races which are more prestigious and carry large purses. Entry into the Derby is reserved to horses that win significant races or carry high totals of graded stakes earnings. In both Florida and California the competition can be fierce. Some young horses can wear themselves out trying to keep pace with so many good ones, or they can injure themselves in their attempts.

If Smarty Jones were going to go to the Kentucky Derby on the first Saturday of May, there were several big hurdles to clear. He would need the wins and earnings that Oaklawn Park in Hot Springs, Arkansas had to offer in their three Derby-prep races, and he would need to correct some bad habits that would otherwise derail his efforts. John knew that Smarty would have been more of a speed demon if he went to Florida, and this problem would be his ruination in longer races. Other issues that needed addressing were running with his head up during races, and the inability of the horse to settle and relax before making his move. Some real tasks were at hand.

When John approached Pat and Chappy about the Arkansas trail, they were surprised. Chappy said, "But we live in Florida, John. Why not send him to Florida?" John's reply was, "You asked me to get you to the Derby." What John went on to explain was, that the path, while unconventional, made more sense for Smarty. They were going to Churchill Downs through the backdoor. John remembered, too, "My dad told me there's no better place in the world to train a racehorse than in Hot Springs. It's quiet, very relaxed, the weather is great, the track is excellent and the people are out of this world."

After settling in during the first few weeks, there appeared to be no real obvious solutions to Smarty's problems. His regular exercise rider Pete Van Trump could manage him, but Pete had returned to Philly, and Smarty was being a bit headstrong with the substitute riders. As the Southwest, the first Oaklawn race, approached, John decided to just "get through this race," before proceeding with a plan. In the Southwest Stakes on Smarty's real birthday, February 28th, his victory was impressive. He had gone one mile in 1:37.2 but John had seen the same charging, that he was trying to correct. As Smarty had hit the backstretch he began to tire, and John wanted to avoid this in future races.

The raceway at Oaklawn Park is a beautiful old facility that has been owned and operated by the Cella Family for over one-hundred years. Neither John Servis nor the Chapmans knew that 2004 was the year of the hundredth anniversary and a special bonus was being offered in conjunction with the celebration. In 1904, C.J.Cella's grandfather had given a $50,000 bonus to the winner of the St. Louis World Fair Stakes. For the Centennial and in memory of his grandfather, C.J. was offering a $5,000,000 dollar bonus to any horse who could win the Rebel Stakes, the Arkansas Derby and the Kentucky Derby. This was a wonderful gesture but a very tall order.

After the Southwest, John and Pete sat down to examine a device that might reel Smarty in a bit without compromising his performance. What they agreed on is called a German Martingale, which is an apparatus that would keep his head down while running and afford greater control to the rider. After one week of use, there was a dramatic change in the horse. He no longer lunged or charged. All of his workouts were decidedly different and the horse seemed at peace with himself. He was more than ready for the next leg, the Rebel Stakes.

On the day of the Rebel Stakes, Chappy was in a Floridian hospital with pneumonia. He remembered that John Servis had told them that Smarty needed to do very well in the Rebel, for the road to the Derby to become a realistic shot. Smarty's competition would be stronger and the race would be longer. It was March 20th and the Arkansas Derby was only three weeks away, with the Kentucky Derby only three weeks after that. Smarty seemed to break well and challenge the other horses. Two of his strongest rivals were Todd Pletcher's Purge and Bob Holthus's Pro Prado. Coming into the stretch, Smarty took the lead and won the mile and one-sixteenth race by 3-3/4 lengths at 1:32 minutes. This victory was crucial in the large scheme and Smarty had just given Chappy some of his best medicine.

The Arkansas Derby is considered a graded stakes race. Prior to this race Smarty had won close to one million dollars but not a penny of it qualified him to go to Churchill Downs. To be part of the twenty-horse field on May 1st, he would have to do very well in the Arkansas Derby, either first or second. Also, to remain in contention for the $5,000,000 Oaklawn Bonus, Smarty needed to win the race outright.

In Smarty's progression among his competition, the Arkansas Derby field would be the most talented that he had ever seen. To complicate things a little more, the track was muddy because of the recent rain. At the start of the race John was uncertain as to how these factors would affect Smarty, but those thoughts became shortlived. Smarty broke well from the gate and then settled in nicely waiting to make his move. When the time came, from two lengths off the pace he took off like a shot. Winning the race by 1-3/4 lengths, he posted a time of 1:49.2 for a mile and an eighth.

Everyone on Team Smarty was more than elated, as the next stop in the magical tour was Churchill Downs on May 1st. For C.J.Cella, the possibility of a $5,000,000 winner was looking a lot more realistic. "When I saw Smarty win the Arkansas…I knew that I needed to get the rest of the bonus insured. There was no way any horse was going to beat Smarty Jones in the Derby," he announced. For Chappy, who missed the Rebel, this was a wonderful memory, "It's unbelieveable to see the way that horse ran today."

For the Philadelphia faithful there were no surprises, just a lot of anticipation of maybe a first place for some team from the City of Brotherly Love. They were more than open to the idea, "Why not Smarty Jones?" For the sportwriters, they had some real catching up to do. Hardly anyone had paid attention to Smarty on a national level. When he finally made it into the Las Vegas line the odds were 75-1. The other more publicized horses were getting a lot of press, but this meant little to John and the others. Just like George Isaacs in Florida, they enjoyed keeping the secret to themselves for as long as possible.

Derby Daze

Someone does not have to be a diehard horseracing fan to enjoy the Kentucky Derby. It has been called, "the greatest two minutes in sports," a title which it has rightly earned over the years. The earliest records of the event indicate that it was run on a piece of land owned by the Churchill brothers, Henry and John. It is the youngest of the three races dubbed Triple Crown races with its origin in 1875. It is here on the first Saturday in May that the best of one year's crop of foals is brought together to compete. There are many traditions, which have been added over the years, and this is part of the charm of the event.

When the Derby first began, there had been a conscious attempt to duplicate the aura which surrounded the Derby Stakes in England. Early Kentucky Derbies were contests of a mile-and-a-half just like the Derby Stakes, but in 1896 the length was shortened to a mile-and-a-quarter. With the Derby Stakes there had always been traditions of stylish clothes and lavish parties. These customs were more aimed at modeling the English race and its accompanying activities, than establishing pure Kentucky Derby traditions in their own right. Over the years these parties have become quite elaborate, and many go on for two weeks. In Louisville, where Churchill Downs is located, there are balls, parades and even steamboat races up and down the Ohio River.

Of the many trappings, which are commonly connected with the Kentucky Derby, there are three traditions that are peculiar to only the Derby and time-honored for many years. In 1853, Stephens Collins Foster wrote the song, "My Old Kentucky Home." This song is very near and dear to the hearts of most Southerners and it is sung as the jockeys and horses make the walk from the paddock. Some of the lyrics reflected another era, and these were changed within the last few years to be more politically correct by today's standards. Few will listen to this singing on Derby Day without feeling an emotional twinge.

The second tradition surrounds the famed mint julep. A julep is characteristically a Southern drink that may be made with a variety of liquors. With the Derby mint julep, earliest sources record a Kentucky farmer adding some spring water to his bourbon and clipping a piece of fresh mint to stir his beverage. Finding these combinations of tastes pleasant, a new cocktail was born. Today's Kentucky Derby juleps are made with good Kentucky bourbon, a sweet syrup (prepared in advance with sugar, boiling water and crushed mint leaves) and are garnished with fresh mint. Since 1948 these have been served at Churchill Downs in the Derby glass of the year. These are highly valued collectibles and most list previous Kentucky Derby winners from Aristides in 1875 to the present. Many will insist that a silver cup is best, because it may be frosted in advance to chill the beverage even more.

If nothing else, the one association that most people make with the Kentucky Derby is the red rose. Strong oral tradition connects the custom of giving roses on Derby Day to socialite E. Barry Wall, who presented roses to his female guests after the race was over back in 1883. This was such a sensation that President Lewis M. Clark established the rose as the official Derby flower. In 1896 pink roses were presented to the winner, Ben Brush; by 1904 the red rose had become the preferred color. By 1925, New York sports columnist Bill Corum dubbed the race as the "Run for the Roses."

The red rose garland as it exists today had its origin in 1932. Since that time 554 individual star roses, complete with water vials and fresh fern, are sewn onto a 2 1/2 yard long by 14 inch wide mantle of green satin with the seal of the Commonwealth of Kentucky at one end and the twin spires of Churchill Downs and the year of the win at the other. Since 1987, the garland has been construct-ed at Kroger Company, a local grocery store chain, on Derby Eve with the pub-lic watching. Prior to that time it was fashioned by the Kingsley Walker Florist, another well known Louisville floral company.

All of these wonderful Derby distractions were only a very small part of the hoopla that was awaiting Smarty Jones and the other entrants as the full festivi-ties of Derby Week kicked in. John Servis, in his wisdom and patience, chose to travel to Keeneland as a prep area for Smarty in the days before the race. It was common knowledge that extensive construction was underway at the Derby site, and that by 2005 the Churchill Downs galleries would have doubled in size. For this moment in May 2004, however, it spelled chaos and confusion. As part of that bigger plan John chose to take his time in getting Smarty Jones there. The colt after all had only been at smaller tracks and calmer venues. This experience was going to be an assault to everyone's nerves.

When John finally made the pilgrimage to the hallowed ground of Churchill Downs, only one week remained before the Derby. Smarty had thoroughly adjusted, loved the accommodations and blazed across the track, turning many heads in the process. After a couple of workouts, even Bob Baffert proclaimed that he was aiming for second, after he had watched the Smarty show. In the *Blood-Horse*, Baffert was quoted as saying, "All I know is that after watching Smarty Jones work today, we're all in trouble." By the second day there, Steve Haskin, from the *Blood-Horse*, remarked, "That was the greatest Derby workout that I have ever seen." Those words rang in as very high praise from someone who had covered the Derby for thirty years. On the other side of the coin, there were the naysayers, who believed that Smarty was the wrong horse, with the wrong trainer, the wrong jockey and the wrong owners. Even with Smarty's record and performance, there were many media folk who criticized everything about the horse. When Smarty Jones went off at 4-1 odds, it was because the people believed in him and connected with his story. One thirteen year old girl named Carly Silver grew weary of hearing Smarty's pedigree trashed by many of the reporters. She wrote a letter tracing his pedigree and sent it to the *Blood-Horse* magazine as a direct challenge to all who were belittling the horse as a "blue-collar horse from the wrong side of the tracks." Even John Servis grew weary of the criticism, "You have no idea how many times I heard, 'He's from Philadelphia; he can't be that good'."

Well, it was just about time for Smarty to strut his stuff Philadelphia mummer-style and dispel the empty charges that he could not measure up to the others. To make the challenge even more difficult, the weather on May 1, 2004 was an abomination with drenching rains and heavy mud everywhere. Through all of this Smarty was being asked to turn things up a notch, and even become a "mudder."

When the time came for the walk to the paddock, everyone was a bit nervous, except Smarty who was taking everything in and loving it. He walked over with a certain air of confidence, even Stew and John seemed to pick up this sense of a "cool, calm and collected Smarty." He knew what was coming, and he was more than ready.

As the field of eighteen charged from the gate, Smarty settled comfortably behind the leader Lion Heart. During most of the mile-and-a-quarter Smarty stayed off the pace and stalked the Lion Heart. All of the while jockey Stewart Elliott knew, "That I had a loaded gun beneath me. He straightened up, switched leads, and I knew it was time to go." With that burst of speed, Smarty would surge past Lion Heart for a two and three-quarter length victory. All that Lion Heart jockey Mike Smith could say was, "I had a great trip and had every opportunity to beat him, but Smarty Jones just had another gear today."

With his dazzling victory, Smarty brought redemption to Team Smarty. It was the first time in twenty-five years that a first-time Derby trainer and first-time Derby jockey had teamed up to win the roses since the team of Spectacular Bid. All of the Philly fans were ecstatic for this was the second Pennsylvania-bred horse to ever win the Derby (previously Lil E. Tee in 1992). Smarty was the fifth undefeated Derby winner in history and the first undefeated Derby winner since

Seattle Slew in 1977. What a day for celebrating big time! To make things a little more special, the $5,000,000 bonus was alive and well. The total earnings for the day were $5,854,800 and this was the largest purse in North America to be awarded for a single race.

For Smarty and his friends, the fairy tale would continue. The horse was shipped back to Philadelphia Park, to assistant trainer Maureen Donnelly, and the rest of the crew, who had been "holding down the fort" in John's absence. Everyone in Philly was so glad to have a winner again; the drought waiting for a bona fide championship of any kind had been very long with no relief in sight until Smarty Jones came along. As John Servis shared with reporters, "Mrs. Chapman said that this horse had actually given Mr. Chapman that extra will to live."....Back in November, Chappy said, "You know that I am not in good health. All I'm asking is to get us to the Derby. So the fact that our team got that done, means everything to me." The crowds would begin to flock to the track every morning to watch Smarty work out as the media descended on a Philadelphia Park, which was anything but ready for the media circus of the next two weeks.

In a way Smarty had become the poster child announcing to the world that dreams do come true and nice things, once in a while, happen to good people. He had overcome insurmountable odds in his short life, as had the people who cared for him. Now he was becoming America's horse, reminiscent of Seabiscuit of the 1930's, and more people were jumping onboard the "Smarty Express" as it made its way to Pimlico. As Pat Chapman told reporters, "This little horse has a lot of fans across this country. I think that this is a great thing for racing." The editors at *Sports Illustrated* thought that it was a good thing for racing, too, as they put Smarty's picture on the cover. This was the first time in almost twenty-five years that a horse's face had graced their cover. Terry McDonell explained,

> Here is this incredible horse coming out of nowhere with beautiful people around him, and he catches the imagination of the entire country. It happens so fast that there comes a moment that you know you have to do it. It was a perfect story, a perfect horse and the right moment. When you have a horse like Smarty Jones, everyone becomes a racing fan.

The Triple Crown Challenge

The term "Triple Crown," as we know it today, dates back to journalist Charles Hatton of the defunct *Morning Telegraph* and present *Daily Racing Form.* As the spring rolled around, Hatton tired of typing the names of the Kentucky Derby, Preakness Stakes and Belmont Stakes. In the early thirties, he coined the phrase "Triple Crown" to describe the three races. Our British friends, "across the pond," had celebrated a series of Triple Crown races for many centuries: the St. Leger (1778 on the Town Moor), the Derby Stakes (1780 at Epsom Downs) and the Two Thousand Guineas (1809 at Newmarket). Here in America, different racing factions struggled to identify three specific races which could become America's Triple Crown.

After the Civil War, aristocrats set out to produce a very fine strain of thoroughbred horses here in the States. Many horses were brought over from England to initiate breeding programs of distinction. Over the next fifty years, these efforts would continue as the pattern of American turfdom took hold. Racing became somewhat centralized in New York, with the states of Maryland, Virginia, Kentucky and Pennsylvania becoming breeding centers. Since Pennsylvania did not exist as a formal racing state, the other states stepped to the forefront with annual races of note.

As thoroughbred breeding programs came into their own, key races became excellent tests of different breeding stock with the hope of improving the breed. The speed of certain thoroughbreds within these races became a predictor of their possible achievement in the breeding shed, in the continuation of certain desired bloodlines.

The President of Churchill Downs in 1875, Colonel Lewis M. Clark grouped three races: the Kentucky Derby, the Key Derby and the Endurance Handicap, and hoped for a large measure of support. In New York, the Withers, the Belmont Stakes and the Lawrence Realization formed a triple challenge to horsemen at the turn of the century. As things began to evolve, neither faction received the support of the other. When Samuel Riddle kept the great Man O' War from the Kentucky Derby, it was more than the youth and immaturity of the horse. Those in the "east" did not wish to travel "west" to Churchill Downs. It would only be when these territorial issues would be settled that the Triple Crown, as we know it today, would exist.

In 1890, the Belmont Stakes and the Preakness Stakes took place on the exact same day, as did the Kentucky Derby and the Preakness in both 1917 and 1922. Situations such as these would make it impossible for one horse to compete in both. There were other times that the patterns were interrupted. In New York between 1911 and 1912, there was a ban on racing of any kind, while the Preakness did not run from 1891 through 1893. Early Preakness Stakes were held in New York, and only formally settled in Maryland by 1908.

As Smarty Jones prepared for the Preakness Stakes as the second jewel in this hallowed crown, there was a great deal of history being made. His wonderful accomplishment at Churchill Downs had finally begun to sink in and the media were in a tizzy. Every major paper in the country was sending correspondents to Philadelphia. No one at Philadelphia Park was really prepared for this onslaught; after all, the track no longer had a press box. At the park, the faithful were coming out in droves. Lines began forming at 5:00 am to watch a Smarty workout. There was a Smarty cake and a huge sign of congratulations on John Servis's Barn 11. Even the track officials were giving Smarty the rare concession of having the track alone from 8:30-8:45 am, with a workout for the public on May 8th. Then on May 13th, Smarty would make the trip to Pimlico in Baltimore.

Once at Pimlico, Smarty seemed to be very relaxed, as if he knew why he was there. Several of the horses that he faced at the Derby would be there, in addition to a number of good competitors, who had been short on their graded earnings, and had missed the Derby. The weather reports appeared to be inconsistent and John wondered if Smarty would face more of the muddy conditions that he had endured at Churchill Downs. Regardless of what was predicted, Smarty was ready to take on this field of nine of the best three-year-olds in the sport.

From the starting gate, Smarty broke very well. Lion Heart quickly went to the lead and Smarty took up his familiar stalking position. Throughout the race, Smarty kept a length or so behind the leader. As the race progressed, Lion Heart seemed to make a wide turn and Stewart took advantage. As Stewart related, "My horse was running so easy, so I just took him to the inside, and he did the rest." As Smarty Jones cut the corner so did Stevens and Rock Hard Ten. It appeared that Rock Hard Ten was the only horse that could spoil the Smarty party. "I was pretty confident at the turn," Stevens added, "because I knew that my horse had an extra gear. I didn't know that Smarty had two more." By this point Smarty was pricking his ears and enjoying everything that was going on. At the same time he was gradually pulling away from the entire field. Before too long, Smarty Jones had buried the field with an eleven and one-half length victory—the longest in the history of the Preakness. The Preakness became known as the "Blowout in Baltimore," as Smarty Jones chalked up one more wonderful victory on the road to the Triple Crown. This race had not been in the plan but John Servis could not have been any happier over Smarty's domination just two weeks after the Derby.

One of the most challenging aspects accompanying the Triple Crown is the pacing of the races. With the British Triple Crown, one race takes place on the first Saturday in May, another in June and the final leg in September. This schedule is much more forgiving, and does not push a horse's endurance to the limit as our Triple Crown does. Of recent memory, very few of the horses running in the Derby will continue with all three races, unless there is a very specific and compelling reason.

After Smarty's "Runaway at Pimlico" the media attention was becoming an obsession. There were three more weeks before the Belmont, and everyone on Team Smarty was ready to move to a deserted island for a couple of days. Chappy announced that he and Pat were thinking of going to Nome, Alaska, to escape the press and the telephone. For a variety of reasons, the American public had taken Smarty into their hearts and he had become their horse. With the war in Iraq and violence within our own country, Smarty's story was an upbeat and positive addition. Everyone in America roots for the underdog and looks for a hero to warmly embrace. In both cases Smarty fit the bill, as the magic continued.

Within the *Daily Racing Form*, esteemed artist and cartoonist, Pierre E. Bellocq presented two large and wonderful illustrations to describe Smarty's journey to Pimlico and his soon-to-be challenge at Belmont Park. In his cartoon, Pimlico had become Oz and the caption read, "There's No Place Like Pimlico." Smarty, munching a large feedbag of Quaker Oats, is pulling an Amish cart with three Amish gentlemen on board (Chappy, Servis and Elliott) as he makes his way down the "yellow brick road." Around the bend, waits the Tin Man (trainer-NickZito), Scarecrow (trainer-Patrick Biancone) and Dorothy (trainer-Kristin Mulhall) to greet them on their way to the Emerald City. With great creativity, Bellocq identified Smarty's Philadelphia and Pennsylvania roots as he tried to keep the magic going.

Another "feel good story" for all Philadelphians is the Rocky story–another underdog whose persistence and hard work brought him to the big time. Bellocq's Smarty stands atop the Philadelphia Art Museum steps in Rocky garb. Each of the pillars of the museum displays the name of a former Triple Crown winner, and the steps leading up list the names of Smarty's competition in the up-and-coming Belmont Stakes. From a distance a very perplexed Lady Liberty looks on, as Smarty raises his boxing gloves (one marked Preakness Stakes and one marked Kentucky Derby) into the air. In the distance, one can see the gallery at Belmont Park. There could not have been a better image to suggest what this contest was going to be like for Smarty Jones and Team Smarty as the days drew near.

Since Affirmed had won the Triple Crown in 1978, there had been no other sweeps. While there were some very serious challenges from nine different horses over the years, there have been no winners. Within the last eight years six different horses had attempted the feat, only to lose at Belmont. Since 1997 trainer Bob Baffert had had three of his colts win the first two races, only to fail at Belmont Park. There are so many simple things that can go wrong, that nothing is ever a sure thing. The great Spectacular Bid stepped on a safety pin, War Emblem stumbled out of the gate and Charismatic broke his leg. In one sense Belmont takes a page out of the Saratoga Book, for Saratoga is always called the "graveyard of champions" because of losses there by Secretariat, Man O' War and others.

In Smarty's Belmont preparation, everything had gone very smoothly. The fans were out in droves and one day almost 9,000 were there for his workout. Even a turf war had evolved in Bensalem, Bucks County, as to whether Smarty was Philly's horse or Bensalem's horse. The mayor of Bensalem, Joseph DiGirolamo, wanted recognition for his 21 square mile township while the Philly fans were starving for a winner after a 21 year drought. Plans were even afoot to change the name of Street Road (outside Philadelphia Park) to Smarty Jones Boulevard. As DiGirolamo related, "Philadelphia is starving for a winner. They can grasp at it, but they need to remember it's in Bensalem and not just Philly." John Servis, a Bensalem resident of many years, sought to resolve the issue, "He's a horse that America loves. I think he belongs to everybody. Everybody can root for this horse. It doesn't matter where you're from." Finally, Sen. Robert Tomlinson of Bucks County put it to rest, "Bensalem is the home of Smarty Jones. But as much as I'd like to claim this horse, he belongs to everyone."

Carrying the hopes and aspirations of the entire country, Smarty Jones made his journey from Pennsylvania to Elmont, New York, the home of Belmont Park, with a police escort. All of his workouts had been great and John felt that he was as ready as he could be. The media stressed that Smarty was going to the Belmont with a bull's eye on his back and that many of his competing jockeys would be seeking ways to spoil the Smarty Party. If Smarty were to win the Triple Crown, another $5,000,000 bonus would be coming his way. If this happened, he would become the largest money winner of all time and eclipse the great Cigar (jockey Jerry Bailey). This would be a challenging feat at best. As Bill Turner, trainer of Triple Crown winner Seattle Slew, remarked,

Whenever you run a horse in a Triple Crown race, and you're the favorite, you don't have to beat one horse, or two horses, you're going to have to beat a combination. You are going to have to beat the speed, and then you are going to have to outstay the stayers, and you accept that going in.

It may have been the first time in history that 120,000 people in New York were rooting for something from Philadelphia—their arch rival (Mike Vaccario—*New York Post*). The Philly Flyer, Smarty Jones, was something very special and he was everyone's horse, even the crowd at Belmont Park. The Smarty Party would continue in Philadelphia, New York and Everywhere USA, if Smarty could pull off the win.

The one and one-half mile distance is daunting at best and none of these three-year-old colts had ever raced at that distance. One secret to a win would be for the jockey to have patience and not to make a move too soon. The distance would be too long for Smarty to make a charge. It was desperately important that he settle in and wait to make one key move at the right time. If it were too early, there would be no more fuel in the tank for the end.

As the race began Smarty broke well and moved to the lead. Normally he would settle back and assume a relaxed position somewhere off of the pace. This was not the case, for he was challenged by some of the horses, who ran early on as hard as they could. In an effort to keep up with them Smarty was forced to run much harder and faster, than either Stew, John or even Smarty himself wanted him to do. Rock Hard Ten (Alex Solis) and Eddington (Jerry Bailey) kept pushing him. As Stewart Elliott remembered, "Usually at this part in the race, he is settled in. He didn't get a chance to get relaxed and settle in." By ganging up on him, Stew could not execute according to the plan. As Dick Jerardi of *The Philadelphia Daily News* most aptly explained,

> They took their horses out of what they did best. They ran early in the race as hard as they could, just to make Smarty run harder and earlier than he really wanted to and forced him into incredibly quick fractions on the back at Belmont Park that could potentially take a toll on Smarty Jones...He got leg weary earlier in the race for the first time in his career.

The race continued with Smarty still leading the charge. His times were very fast, but it was obvious by his shortened strides that he was tiring. On the outside and almost out of nowhere, came Birdstone (Edgar Prado), the 36-1 long shot. If the race had been three lengths shorter Smarty probably would have won, but he could not compete with a charging Birdstone. For the first time Smarty had lost a race and Belmont Park went totally silent for at least 45 seconds. No one could believe that Smarty had lost; Birdstone was first, and Rock Hard Ten and Eddington were out of the money. It appeared that the bull's eye theory was accurate and Smarty would not allow himself to settle regardless of Stew's efforts. Another staff writer for *The Philadelphia Inquirer,* Don Steinberg, offered this explanation, "(Smarty) barely lost the Belmont Stakes in June–a victim, experts said, of opposing jockeys' willingness to sacrifice their own chances in order to tire him out early." He was used to leading the pack but not at that distance. The race had taken its toll, in more ways than one.

A Different Kind of Race Begins

In the weeks separating the Preakness and the Belmont, Pat and Chappy were meeting with many of the presidents and owners from some of the most prestigious breeding operations in central Kentucky. Even if Smarty would return to race in his fourth year, it was key that a farm be chosen for his next career as a breeding stallion, whenever that would be. It would be in the best interests of all of these farms to secure a stunning champion who was moving closer and closer to greatness. "It's fair to say that every farm in the country, if not the world, is interested in Smarty Jones," said Dan Rosenberg, president of Blythe and Robert Clay's Three Chimneys Farm, in Midway, Kentucky.

In addition to Three Chimneys Farm, some of the other interested farms included: Coolmore's Ashford Stud near Versailles, Darley at Jonabell near Lexington, Hill 'n' Dale near Versailles, Taylor Made Farm near Nicholasville, Lane's End near Versailles, Vinery near Lexington, Walmac International near Lexington and WinStar Farm near Versailles.

This region of Central Kentucky is very well suited to the breeding of horses. The lush and rich vegetation of the Bluegrass, with its limestone base and high concentration of phosphorus, lends itself to raising strong and healthy horses. In the area alone there are over 500 thoroughbred horse farms with more than 30,000 broodmares.

Early in Smarty's development, the man who saw the magic before anyone else was George Isaacs. At another significant point in Smarty's career, the Chapmans would once again turn to their trusted friend to help them sort through the various offers and bargaining pieces that were being passed across the table. There were several issues that were very important to the Chapmans. If Smarty were America's horse, Pat believed that Smarty must not leave the country. As a continuation of that thought, both Pat and Chappy wanted him in a setting that was accessible to the public. Some farms offer tours on a regular basis; others remained closed to the public.

This was not an easy decision for the Chapmans as each farm offered something unique to complement Smarty's talent and personality. When the final decision was made, it would be Three Chimneys Farm in Midway, Kentucky. Upon his arrival, Smarty would be occupying the same stall as had previously belonged to the Triple Crown great, Seattle Slew.

Both Pat and Chappy were pleased with the arrangements that Dan Rosenberg and Blythe and Robert Clay had laid out for Smarty's stallion career. He would stand at Three Chimneys for a stud fee of $100,000 which would be predicated on a live foal. During one year's breeding season, Smarty would be bred to 111 mares, which was an average number as far as breedings go. Before a contract would be offered an assessment of the mare's background/ pedigree/race record would be done. For Smarty to be bred to a particular mare, it would be necessary that this union would enhance Smarty's record by producing a foal with a strong proclivity toward racing. Only a strong pedigree match would be a choice for such a breeding.

The farm, that would be Smarty's new home, had been purchased thirty-two years before by Blythe and Robert Clay. At that time it had been a mere 100 acres and an undeveloped cattle farm complete with a tobacco barn. The Clays rolled up their sleeves and created a wonderful breeding operation with a large amount of good hard work and a standard of superior and ethical performance. Their motto is, "The idea is excellence," and its actualization can be seen in all facets of the farm.

By 2004, Three Chimneys had amassed a total of 1,700 acres. The first stallion to stand here was Slew of Gold in 1984, soon to be followed by his undefeated Triple Crown winning sire, Seattle Slew. From that time on the operation has grown tremendously. On the total property there are 14 stallions, 175 yearlings, 400 broodmares and 300 new foals. The farm employs approximately 150 people and conducts its business on six different continents with an office in Japan.

The Chapmans were more than comfortable with their choice for Smarty when his stallion career would come to fruition. Plans were in place to race him locally through the summer, then off to Lone Star for the Breeders' Cup in the fall. Many of the stipulations surrounding Smarty racing as a four-year-old depended on John Servis whom the Chapmans were entrusting with that decision.

Farewell to Smarty

In the days following the Belmont Stakes, Smarty Jones didn't seem to gallop with the same gusto. The length and intensity of Smarty's seven and one-half month campaign had taken its toll. Since the previous November, the feisty chestnut colt had made the rounds from Pennsylvania to New York, then on to four months in Arkansas, on route to Churchill Downs, Pimlico and Belmont Park. By the spring of 2004, Smarty had covered a tremendous amount of ground in his bid for the Derby, considering that less than a year before he almost killed himself in a starting gate accident. The colt had recuperated through the late summer and early fall before winning his maiden at Philadelphia Park on November 9th.

Smarty was afforded some much-deserved rest after the Belmont Stakes, while John Servis and the Chapmans projected ahead with some possible racing venues for Smarty during the late summer and early fall. With good progress and sufficient rest Smarty would be entered in both the Travers at Saratoga and the Pennsylvania Derby at his own home Philadelphia Park. Another fall target would be the Breeders' Cup at Lone Star Park in Texas. All of these plans were contingent on Smarty's full recovery from his sore feet and legs.

The staff at Philadelphia Park was anticipating a huge crowd for the Pennsylvania Derby, and were realistically assessing exactly, "How many people could the place hold?" If the magic number were 35,000, there were many logistical details which needed to be addressed, including extra bleachers, air-conditioned tents, more parking and larger purses.

During the last week of July John Servis noticed that Smarty had a bruised left hoof. As Pat Chapman confirmed, "There is a bruise just on the left hoof. He had been a little tender before the Derby, but I don't know if it's related." The nature of the injury was such that Smarty would not physically be ready for participation in the Pennsylvania Derby over Labor Day weekend. This was a great disappointment to all at Philadelphia Park and the Philly fan base as well.

Over the next few days opinions were sought from a number of veterinary specialists. One of the veterinarians was Dr. Roger Clymans of Philadelphia Park. After a series of radiographs (X-rays) had been done, Dr. Clymans noted, "Unremarkable, but the diagnostic nerve blocks which were done indicated that the problem was with the ankles." The horse was then taken to Dr. Peter Bousum at the Mid-Atlantic Equine Medical Center in Ringoes, New Jersey. While at the equine hospital, Smarty underwent a high-tech scintigraphic evaluation to determine the severity of his injuries. The scintigraphy showed that Smarty had micro cracks from intense bone stress to such a degree that the healing process was unable to keep up with the damage to all four legs. The horse had breezed at such high speeds over a series of months that the stress had become overwhelming. Smarty's feet no longer had the cushioning effect necessary to absorb the rigors of training or the shock of racing.

When all of the analyses had been done, it was clear that Smarty Jones's injuries were far more serious than originally noted. His retirement was announced on the 2nd of August, 2004. This was a very unpopular decision for many of his fans, but the campaign had exacted its toll on a very dynamic horse that was experiencing serious and possibly permanent setbacks because of it. He could not continue to race in his present state.

For many, the timing of the retirement was more than people could handle. As Dick Jerardi sensitively identified, "The timing of the retirement was terrible, because it was right after the Belmont Stakes. I can't say that he didn't have a significant injury, because I have been told he did by people whose experience I trust." As Pat Chapman added, "None of us is happy about this retirement because I believe that people think he had a lot more to prove. To us, we think that he already proved a lot.... We think far beyond the track, it became part of a growing national legend affecting Americans of every age and walk of life." Since this kind of decision is constantly open to speculation, there were many people who had experience in this type of endeavor, and shared their wisdom. As Bill Turner (Seattle Slew's trainer) said, "If the horse had problems and he wasn't going to be as good a horse coming back, they made a wise decision."

A public Retirement Party for Smarty Jones was held at Philadelphia Park on Saturday, August 14, 2004, between the third and fourth races. Fans came in droves to bid farewell and good luck to a special horse that was having a love affair with the American public. As expected, more than 10,000 people showed up sporting Smarty tee shirts, hats, buttons and pictures. For most it was a bittersweet moment because many of these fans never expected to see Smarty up-close-and-personal again. As Doris Cichonke, of Philadelphia, told the *Inquirer*, "If I didn't come here to see him, I would have regretted it for the rest of my life."

The afternoon ceremony consisted of a few speakers who thanked the thousands of fans for their support. Everyone wished Smarty well as he would be transported in the next few days to Three Chimneys Farm in Midway, Kentucky for stallion duties in 2005. Sen. Robert Tomlinson "thanked Smarty for a great ride." Another unspoken thank you from the Senator may have identified

Smarty's role in propelling the state legislature to legalize slots machines at the track. John Servis, Smarty's trainer, had journeyed to Harrisburg to implore legislators to permit the slots to financially rejuvenate purses and track conditions. In his speech, Servis praised Smarty's dynamic efforts which made him the champion that he is. He also reminded fans that, "We're doing what's in the best interest of him, and that's what you have to look at. We have to look out for this horse. We're going to miss him."

At the conclusion of the winner's circle activities, Smarty was walked back to Barn 11 by exercise rider Pete Van Trump and groom Mario Arriaga. There was a bit of a farewell party planned there which would be emotional for everyone involved. Smarty's journey was remarkable and had been nothing less than spectacular. He had put Philadelphia Park on the NTRA (National Thoroughbred Racing Association) radar screen in a special and undeniable way. There were new fans of racing from all walks of life because of Smarty and his charisma. The industry needed a first-class shot in the arm, and here it was coming from a Pennsylvania born and bred.

For John, Maureen, Pete, Bill, Mario and the others, this was going to be a very trying moment to say good-bye to Smarty Jones. He was the "little shrimp," who had arrived at Philadelphia Park, taken their world by surprise and turned it into a magical experience. What he had accomplished in a few months was beyond comprehension and his effect on everyone nothing short of brilliant. He would be making his way to Three Chimneys Farm that evening in a very large and comfortable horse van and a whole new world would be opening up for him. As Smarty took his place on board, Pat Chapman and John Servis took one more look at their champion, and with a large lump in their throats and tears in their eyes closed the door to the van.

Smarty Jones was foaled on Pat and Roy Chapman's Someday Farm on February 28, 2001. Farm manager, Deb Given, helped to give that extra tug that brought Smarty to see the light of day. His dam I'll Get Along enjoyed romping with her quick and agile colt during his early months on the farm in West Grove, Chester County, Pennsylvania.

Smarty Jones was stabled and trained at the barn of John C. Servis at Philadelphia Park in Bensalem, Pennsylvania (top right). Exercise rider, Peter Van Trump, met some challenges as he settled the young Smarty Jones and channeled his great speed (bottom right). Pat Chapman and granddaughter, Alexandrea, take a few minutes to treat Smarty to a carrot in his stall at Philly Park (above).

Groom, Mario Arriaga, leads Smarty to the Paddock at Churchill Downs for the Kentucky Derby.

Smarty Jones scores a dramatic victory in the 130th Kentucky Derby, and just two short weeks later buries his competition at the Preakness Stakes. Described by some reporters as the "Blowout in Baltimore," Smarty scored the largest margin of victory in the history of the Preakness--eleven and one-half lengths. In a press conference following Smarty's victory in the 130th Kentucky Derby, May 1, 2004, Pat and Roy (Chappy) Chapman chat with media.

Smarty Jones III is shown by artist Pierre E. Bellocq as another of Philadelphia's sons, Rocky III. Pictured with Smarty on the pillars of the Philadelphia Museum of Art are the names of the Triple Crown Winners of yesteryear, and on the steps leading up are the names of his opponents in the 2004 Belmont Stakes. Even one of Pennsylvania's Amish Farmers is around the corner (left) to wish Smarty luck.

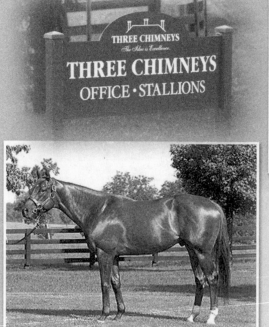

Smarty Jones traveled to Three Chimneys Farm in Midway, KY in August 2004 to begin his new career as a stallion. Since that time, thousands have traveled to visit him there as part of the daily tours which the farm conducts. In January of 2006, the first Smarty Jones foal was born on Stone Farm in Paris, Kentucky. The yearling filly, whose name is Saayebah, resides at Shadwell Farm.

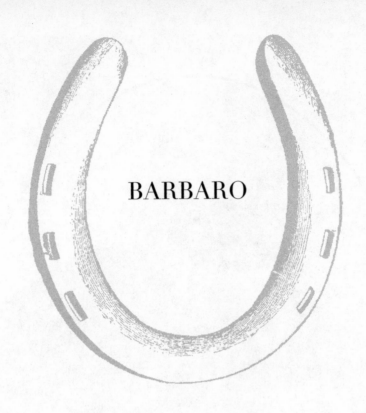

BARBARO

*"He is greatest whose strength carries up
the most hearts by the attraction of his own."*
- H.W. Beecher

Pennsylvania Traditions

The beautiful countryside of southeastern Pennsylvania has been the site of many rich and stately horse farms. In the late nineteenth century, the great horseman Samuel Riddle chose some of these picturesque and rolling hills for his famous Glen Riddle Farm, named for his family's earliest roots in Scotland. Among Riddle's famous contributions to thoroughbred racing were the legendary Man O' War, 1937 Triple Crown Winner War Admiral and English Grand National Winner Battleship. Probably remembered most for his dour persona in the Seabiscuit v. War Admiral Match Race, Riddle established a rich racing tradition that exists today more in bloodlines than in historical sites.

Over the years many outstanding thoroughbreds have had their origins in Pennsylvania. Among these are Danzig, Storm Cat, Go For Wand, Lil E. Tee and Smarty Jones. As a racehorse, Danzig was undefeated in a short career ending prematurely due to knee joint injuries. He later became one of the world's most prolific sires. Another impressive progeny is Storm Cat. As one of the leading sires in North America, his fee for a live foal is currently at $500,000. The outstanding filly Go For Wand was the winner of the 1989 Breeders' Cup Juvenile Fillies and the 1990 Eclipse Award for Outstanding Three-Year-Old Filly. During a much touted match against Bayakoa, an Argetinian mare, Go For Wand broke down in the 1990 Breeders' Cup Distaff before a national audience. In a painful moment reminiscent of Ruffian, Go For Wand was euthanized on the track after dragging herself to finish the race. She was inducted into the National Museum of Racing and Hall of Fame in 1996 as a much-deserved honor. Other Pennsylvania success stories, both Lil E. Tee and Smarty Jones list Kentucky Derby wins among their accomplishments, and Smarty also triumphed in the Preakness Stakes.

While not rivaling the deep Kentuckiana horse tradition, Pennsylvania has commanded a formidable presence especially in the last five years. With the advent of Smarty Jones and his pursuit of the Triple Crown in 2004, and the dynamics of Afleet Alex in the Triple Crown races of 2005, the Delaware Valley had taken a big stake in the action. After Afleet Alex's would-be fall and remarkable recovery in the Preakness victory of 2005, a local Philadelphia newspaper's very large headlines read, "WE HAVE HORSES! WE HAVE HORSES!" Many of the Pennsylvania faithful were still relishing Smarty's victories, and wanted to believe that lightning could strike twice in the same place. From the Preakness Stakes, Afleet Alex soared on to Belmont Park and recorded one of the most dramatic victories there since the great days of Secretariat. In 2004 and then again in 2005, Smarty and Alex had come so close to capturing the elusive Triple

Crown and "racing fever" was gaining some newly-found momentum in the Keystone State. Although the fans were poised for a winner, few, if any, would have suggested that Philadelphia was about to hit the Trifecta with a very special horse that was just around the corner. On the other hand, wouldn't it have been something special? After all, "Three's a charm!"

A Star is Born

In 1978, Gretchen and Roy Jackson chose to pull-up stakes in Chester Springs, Chester County, Pennsylvania and move their farm to the other side of the county. A school chum of Roy's, Russell Jones, had shared the tip that the lovely farm near his home was "For Sale," and the Jacksons jumped at the news. All of Chester County's sprawling green hills are welcoming to horse-lovers, but this section of the tri-state area is particularly inviting.

The beautiful 190-acre Lael (Gaelic for loyalty) Farm has been home to the Jackson's animal family for thirty years. Any visitor will encounter retired horses, cows, ponies, miniature donkeys, sheep and dogs. During the first twenty years in this southern Chester County hamlet of West Grove, the Jacksons specialized in foaling, boarding and breaking horses. It is only within the last six or seven years that they began to gather a solid broodmare foundation and to engage more deeply in thoroughbred racing.

Many of their successes in the early years of 2000 were overseas with English trainers, James Fanshawe and William Haggas. Some of their stars included: Superstar Leo, an English and French champion, Belle Cherie and C'Est L' Amour, both of which were North American grade II winners. Another winner for them was Grandera who raced well in Europe as a two and three year old. He was on his way to bigger-and-better things but the distance factor made it difficult for the Jacksons to attend races and participate in training. After a private sale to Godolphin Racing, he went on to win three grade I stakes races. It was his half brother, George Washington, racing in England, who won the Stan James Two Thousand Guineas (Eng-I) on May 6, 2006, the equivalent of the first leg of our Triple Crown.

With the Jacksons' decision to engage in racing to a greater extent, Lael Farm was moving away from a full-scale operation, and the Jacksons were seeking desirable broodmares to add to their growing band. While making this transition, they received a welcomed call from Kathy Ringert, a bloodstock agent based at Fairhill Training Center in Maryland. It seemed that a Carson City mare, La Ville Rouge, of Maycroft Farm was up-for-sale and her background would later prove to be somewhat unique. The Jacksons were pleased with her potential and made the sale. "We've tried all along to find horses with a good-enough family," shared Gretchen, "she (Ringert) just knew of her as a two-year-old that was up for sale." Her sire Carson City was a renowned sire of great sprinters, but LaVille would go on to place in four graded stakes races between eight and eleven furlongs on dirt and turf—a feat that later made her an even more desirable dam.

In examining possible breeding options for La Ville, some consideration was given to investing in stamina, as her sire had been known for his great speed. Breeding is a science in its own regard, although not an exact science. One can do exhaustive research, plot a desirable course and be terribly surprised by the results. While there are no guarantees, a careful examination of the depth and strengths of the pedigree may mean a great deal.

During the planning of their breeding and racing efforts, the Jacksons have surrounded themselves with experts. Approximately five years ago they were introduced to Headley Bell, a well known bloodstock agent who began advising the couple on good choices. The Carson City mare La Ville was deemed to be of average size but not heavy bodied. Bell's suggestion was to send her to a stallion who would add some size to the equation. The choice was made; it would be Dynaformer, son of Roberto out of Andover Way.

As a stallion, Dynaformer had been a star in his own right, but it had not come overnight. He had entered stud at Wafare Farm for a modest fee of $5,000. Through the years he had worked his way up and now commanded a more formidable presence at Robert Clay's Three Chimneys Farm. At the time of the breeding the fee was $50,000 and this match was viewed as a desirable wedding of two premier lines. La Ville's sire was Carson City, whose grand sire was Mr. Prospector, whose grand sire was Native Dancer. Native Dancer had been known for his come-from-behind style and missed the Triple Crown by a hair at the Kentucky Derby. He was viewed by many as a very desirable stud. For this reason it was believed that these bloodlines ran strong, and they coupled well with the Roberto line by Hail to Reason.

The grand sire of Dynaformer, Hail to Reason, had been a rising star. He had been the 1960 Best Two-Year-Old Male, owned by Hirsch Jacobs and Isidor Bieber, and raced in the name of Jacobs' daughter, Patrice. He had won the Hopeful Stakes, the Great American, Sanford, Sapling, Tremont, World's Playground and Youthful Stakes up through September. He was well on his way when a terrible disaster struck. At Aqueduct, Hail to Reason took a bad step and fractured both sesamoids in his left front leg. As an instantaneous response, Jacobs and his son John grabbed the horse's leg and prevented a further misstep. The son held the injured horse's leg as the father prepared a plaster of Paris cast. It was an early Sunday morning and there were no vets around to assist. This seemingly small intervention saved the horse and turned the history of racing/breeding for years to come. As John stated,

> I grabbed his leg. Father had me hold it up so he wouldn't step down on his ankle. There were no vets around that early on Sunday, so we had no tranquilizers at that time. When we got him back to the stall, Father rolled a plaster of Paris cast on the leg. I think the horse knew how seriously he was hurt, because he stood like a statue when we put the cast on.

The culprit was thought to be a loose shoe that was found nearby. This intervention by the Jacobs saved the horse's life, but the future prognosis was held in the balance for many weeks. The cast cracked several times but the horse remained docile the entire time. "He'd never fight you or struggle with you, so you had an easy time nursing him back," related John Jacobs. The ups-and-downs of the injury continued for several months and by the fall of 1961 the horse was returned to Dr. Charles Hagyard's farm in Lexington, where he had been foaled. It was this single chapter and the Jacobs' quick response that would later alter the course of breeding history.

Under Hagyard's care, Hail to Reason entered stud in 1961. One of the original shareholders at $35,000 was leading breeder/owner, John Galbreath. From this business venture would come many desirable colts and fillies. Hail to Reason sired Roberto (European classic winner and champion), Prince Thou Art (first to upset Foolish Pleasure-Florida Derby 1975) and Proud Clarion (1967 Kentucky Derby Winner). It was through his offspring that he completed a Triple Crown of sorts. In 1970, his son Personality won the Preakness Stakes, Champion Three-Year-Old Male, and co-Horse-of-the-Year honors. Another son, Hail to All, would capture the 1965 Belmont Stakes. With these wins it makes one wonder what Hail to Reason would have accomplished had he not been injured.

One of Galbreath's equine stars was Roberto, who had much to live up to as a racehorse and stud. As owner of the Pittsburgh Pirates, Galbreath had named Roberto after Hall of Famer, Roberto Clemente. The European champion Roberto won the Epsom Derby (Eng-I) and the Benson and Hedges Gold Cup (Eng-I). In 1971 he was named Ireland's champion 2-year-old male and later, as a four year old, he would take the Coronation Cup (Eng-I). Later in stud he would produce a wonderful line of 86 stakes winners who were able to go the distance. From his 1985 crop would come Dynaformer, a skilled runner who excelled on dirt and turf.

The Jacksons arranged for La Ville to go to Dynaformer in 2002 in a mating that would later produce Barbaro. After researching the pedigrees, they believed that the speed of the Carson City line sired by Mr. Prospector coupled with the stamina of the Hail to Reason line would work well together. With the depth of talent shared by both sire and dam, the colt would later prove to be as versatile as his parents.

On April 29, 2003 little LaVille was foaled at Sanborn Chase near Nicholasville, Kentucky. Interestingly enough both Sandy and Bill Sanborn will relate that he was anything but little. His dam wasn't very large herself and needed help from Bill Sanborn and Irvin White, the night watchman/assistant. Both men had to roll up their sleeves and pull a very lanky foal from his mother. After that initial effort the mare and foal did well.

The little LaVille colt and his mother remained at Sanborn Chase as he adjusted to life with the other mares and foals. White recalled, "We had a group of foals, but he was always different from the rest." Everyone at the farm took a liking to him and his easy-going way endeared him to many of the trainers. For Sally Mullis, who worked with him in the foaling and yearling barn, "He was just a nice little bay colt. He chimed right in and got with the program. He was never a troublemaker." Keith Ritchie found his disposition to be equally as pleasant, "He was so mild-mannered, I could roll him over on his back and scratch his belly or pick out his feet….He was real brawny and had the nicest temperament."

When he was weaned in the fall of 2003, he joined a group of five or six other colts. They would romp and play together, but as White recalled, "He was always the leader of the pack." Over time his nature did not change for he always liked people. "I always spent more time with him, because he'd stand right there and let you rub on him," White related, "But he'd never eat one of my peppermints."

Many of the colts and fillies in the Sanborns' care were going to be sold. These would roam freely with the Jacksons' horses, and early on these became much more socially adjusted than other animals which were kept separately. In a group they would rear and jump and play together. "It makes you worry, but, to me, it's the best way to raise them," Sanborn recalled. "You'll have a lot less stall vices, and vices period, if you can keep them together. Because once you separate them out, you're the only playmate they've got."

In this environment the La Ville foal progressed nicely. He would remain there until it became time to go to Ocala, Florida to John Stephenson's farm to be broken and begin racehorse school. After the move he would no longer be the LaVille foal or colt but he would be called Barbaro. This name originated in an heirloom painting that Gretchen and Roy Jackson found in Roy's mother's attic after her death. There are five foxhounds in the painting and each is named. The one in the lower right corner is "Barbaro," and Gretchen Jackson selected that name for the foal. The rest is history....

Team Barbaro

As Gretchen and Roy Jackson approached the Winner's Circle at Churchill Downs on May 6, 2006, it must have seemed like the best of dreams had come true. Some say that, "Good things come in threes," and for them that day it was true. In the morning a horse of their breeding, George Washington, had won the Stan James English Two Thousand Guineas (Eng-I) at Newmarket, an equivalent of our Kentucky Derby. Later that afternoon, they watched their two undefeated horses Showing Up and Barbaro compete in the 132nd Kentucky Derby with Barbaro winning the roses. That is more good fortune than any thoroughbred breeder could wish for in a lifetime.

For the Jacksons it has been more than a career with horses, although the involvement has taken many different forms. For Gretchen Schaefer Jackson, originally of Chestnut Hill, horses had been a part of her life for as long as she could remember. At the age of four, she sported pictures of the great Whirlaway, the Triple Crown Winner that year (1941). "I dreamed of having racehorses, or at least having a horse...I wanted to be like Elizabeth Taylor in 'National Velvet,'" Gretchen recalled. In elementary school and through early adolescence, she took lessons at the Violet Haines Riding Camp in Gwynedd Valley. Through Miss Haines's tutelage, she attended and participated in many local horse shows— Devon and the like. She remembers, "I did anything to be around a horse." Her particular interest became foxhunting which she actively pursued in many local venues including Huntingdon Valley, Pickering, Radnor and Andrews Bridge. Her involvement with thoroughbreds grew as an adjunct to her hunting.

After attending Springside School in Chestnut Hill from kindergarten through twelfth grade, she moved on to the University of Pennsylvania. Throughout her childhood and later adolescence, she also took a very active interest in all forms of sports. Among her favorites were field hockey, lacrosse and basketball in which she found her highly competitive side. Many of these athletic interests carried over to Penn, but became short-lived as academics became dominant through her sophomore year.

After her graduation from the University of Pennsylvania in 1959, she taught kindergarten for one year. The desire to assist those who are in need was a natural outgrowth of her love for children. It would be years later that she would attend Neumann College and complete a Masters degree in Pastoral Counseling. Some of her ministries have included: the Mirmont Care Center (nine years of working with the children of drug and alcohol parents), Y.M.C.A. (acting as a drug and alcohol prevention specialist with elementary age children) and Tressler Agency (counseling on a sliding scale in the Wilmington, Delaware area). Her care and concern for animals can be seen, too, as a further outgrowth of her ministry. As she has said many times, "Horses work for you and you have a responsibility to take care of them." Later developments would see this apostolate of sorts extended to horses at New Bolton Center of the University of Pennsylvania Veterinary School near her home in West Grove, Pennsylvania.

Within her busy schedule Gretchen Jackson seems to find time for some very worthwhile volunteer projects. She recently received "The Award for Distinguished Service" from Springside School, where she serves on the Board of Trustees. Other boards which receive a large measure of her attention are: The Thoroughbred Charities of America, the University of Pennsylvania Veterinary School and Anna House (a day-care facility for the children of backstretch employees at Belmont Park). "Whether it's TCA or Anna House or a new foundation we choose to create, we really want to do something because we've been so fortunate," Jackson related.

During her junior year at Springside, Gretchen met the love-of-her life Roy Jackson at a dance at the Merion Tribute House. "It was one of the subscription dances, where we'd pay $100 a year to go to five dances," she recalled. Their courtship continued through their years together at Penn. In 1959 Gretchen and Roy were married at St. Thomas Church in Chestnut Hill, not too far from Gretchen's childhood home. The Jacksons have four children: MacRoy, Lucy, Hardie, Fred and a brood of eleven grandchildren.

Horses have also occupied a key part of M. Roy Jackson's life in a somewhat different way. As a native of Edgemont, Delaware County, Roy's father Roy Sr. was the Master of the Hounds for Rose Tree and Radnor in the '30s and '40s. He also bred a new foxhound called the Pennmarydel which today has become a popular breed among foxhunters. After the death of his father, Roy's mother married a noted Philadelphia attorney Hardie Scott. The couple acquired a few mares from Elizabeth Arden Graham's Maine Chance Farm which they kept at Crestfield Farm in Kentucky. Locally they raced their horses at Delaware Park, Atlantic City and several Maryland tracks. "They were into racing, not the breeding side," Roy noted. It wouldn't be until the late '90s that Gretchen and Roy would move into serious breeding themselves.

Possessing sharp business acumen, Roy Jackson has moved well in several different business avenues. Initially he spent six years as a stockbroker. After a friend introduced him to Bob Carpenter of the Philadelphia Phillies, his life took another turn. Baseball had always been his passion but a heart operation in college had restricted his playing. This new contact brought a new direction, "Mr. Carpenter started a business training program to bring younger people into the game.... I worked with the Phillies' minor league clubs for nearly two years before the opportunity arose to purchase the Class AA York Pirates and become the club president," Roy explained. He would later sell the franchise and be named President of the Eastern League. In 1972, he launched two new AAA clubs which he later sold. Next he would run the Pacific Coast League and the International League from 1975-82, before launching a Sports Agency Firm called Convest. He would remain with Convest from 1983-2001.

Since the late' 90s both Jacksons have followed their hearts into the thoroughbred arena. After early modest successes, they have now stepped on to the international stage and are enjoying the view very much. With their number one quality horses, chances are they will be a formidable presence in the industry for some time

Even the best-bred horses can fail in their racing efforts if not guided by a quality trainer. It is the trainer who enters the mind of the horse and knows its strengths and weaknesses. One of greatest racing dynasties of the past, Calumet Farm in the '40s, was built by the efforts of one very skilled trainer, Ben A. Jones. His ability to assess a particular horse's talent and potential was worth its weight in gold.

From Barbaro's earliest days at Sanborn Chase, the Jacksons sensed that there was something unique and possibly precocious about the bay colt. He was a strong and determined leader that also had an usual warmth toward and acceptance of the humankind. He seemed to enjoy the personal contact and behind those intelligent eyes lurked a competitive spirit. His greatest chance at success on the racetrack would come to fruition if placed in the hands of a very special and knowing trainer. For Gretchen and Roy Jackson that special person would be Michael Matz.

In his road to becoming a thoroughbred trainer, Michael Matz had not taken the conventional path. It is not the least bit novel for a trainer to have grown up around horses, to share family in the profession or to have been a former jockey. For Michael Matz none of these connections existed. He was the son of a plumber from Shillington, Pennsylvania, who was headed for Albright College but never made it.

As a teenager, Michael worked for his father's friend on a farm near Adamstown, Pennsylvania. The owner had purchased two horses, one for him and one for his wife. After the wife's refusal to ride, he turned to Michael, who had never been on a horse. After several weeks of cantering and one aerial ride, compliments of the horse, Michael became hooked. He joined a pony club, attended shows and changed jobs. Picking up with show rider Bernie Taurig in Mechanicsville, PA, he worked for two different farms over the next several years. After that he went on to riding with J. Basil Ward before moving to the Dixon's Farm in Lafayette Hill, Pennsylvania. When Michael made the American show-jumping team, he had only been on a horse for seven years. It would be three more years before he would be going to his first Olympics in Lucerne.

Those who have ridden in equestrian competition will tell you that you must get into the horse's mind. In the competition you move as one; both rider and horse are in sync as they ride through the course and into the jumps. It takes a special gift to sense the animal's needs and apprehensions and to restore the perfect equilibrium which is required. Over the years Michael Matz has acquired that sensitivity to lead his horses to the next level. He perceives what others may not. "Each horse is different and has a different personality. A good trainer can work in different disciplines; you just have to make adjustments. People have different personalities and so do the horses," related Matz. In the profession his colleagues would say that "Matz trains outside the box." Over the years he has cultivated his own style and it is one of perfection. Each decision is the result of careful thought and analysis gleaned from his experience. He doesn't do what is expected but what he thinks is best. His barn, his staff, his horses and his world speak to order, discipline and precision. Everything that guided his life as a disciplined, successful Olympian athlete, now directs his efforts as a trainer. He reflects the pristine perfection of his life's goals in his work.

During his life, Michael Matz has had his share of defining moments— catapulting into the horse world, carrying the US flag at the Olympics, winning a silver medal in Atlanta and claiming victory in the 132nd Kentucky Derby. Few, if any, can compare with the happenings of July 19, 1989 when United Flight 232 crashed in a Sioux City, Iowa cornfield killing 112 of the 295 passengers onboard.

Matz and his fiancé D.D. Alexander were able to flee the burning craft but not before Matz gathered up the three young Roth children, who were flying to visit their grandmother in Albany. He led them from the plane and then returned to rescue a baby that someone had heard crying. The burning fuselage had flipped over and broken in two and the baby was caught in the luggage area. After returning to the plane, Matz forced opened the compartment and handed the baby to a nearby woman. As Matz shared, "I believe a lot in fate....when the airplane blew up, I never thought that I would die that way. I guess that I wasn't supposed to." From that sobering experience to everything that Michael Matz does, he does it in a first class way. As his fiancé D.D. explained, "It's about caring for others and not yourself first."

When Barbaro romped in the 132nd Kentucky Derby, Michael Matz wanted everyone to know that the horse was the true star. "Good horses make good riders and good horses make good trainers," he said. Veteran horsemen would agree with Matz but also suggest that it has a lot to do with the jockey. The relationship which exists between the horse and his rider has everything to do with the outcome. An astute trainer will make every effort to complement the horse's style with an experienced jockey. As Barbaro had met with initial successes in his early races, it became apparent that a more experienced jockey could guide his efforts in the more challenging stakes races that would be over the horizon. For this task, Michael Matz and the Jacksons enlisted the veteran Edgar Prado.

It had been twenty years since Edgar Prado had left Peru for America, and he had made his mark on the racing world. He was listed among the top twenty most-winning jockeys of all time. But none of this could have ever happened, if he had not followed his dream. As the second youngest in a family of 12 children, Edgar was hesitant about trying to find his fortune in the United States. His mother Cenaida was his greatest cheerleader who prodded him to continue when the going became rough. There are a lot of racetracks in the United States and a plethora of jockeys. Breaking into the sport on the highest level can be a very difficult task, if not an impossible one. His mother kept his spirits buoyed and was there for Edgar throughout his career. As he garnered a measure of success, she would come to the United States to visit and share his good fortune as he progressed in the sport.

By the late' 90s Edgar had made a name for himself, earning top jockey honors three years in a row from 1997-1999. Riding in many of the Triple Crown races over the years, he had won both the Preakness and the Belmont Stakes. For some reason the quintessinal prize of all, the Kentucky Derby, had eluded him. In a way it was bothersome not to capture the roses of the race-of-all-races, as a

Dan Marino of jockeys waiting for his first Super Bowl victory. It was his reputation for strength and determination which would keep him in the forefront and eventually give him the Derby prize.

He had chosen to stay with the East Coast racetracks and he made his home in southern Florida. Over the years he had amassed a following of first class trainers and owners, who recognized his courage and tenacity on the track. He had also demonstrated a caring spirit as he bonded with many of his rides. This level of care would bring him to form a relationship with Barbaro, based on an understanding of kindred spirits. The horse's greatest accomplishments would be under the reins of Edgar Prado.

As 2005 was drawing to a close, Edgar's mother Cenaida would be diagnosed with breast cancer. To provide the best possible medical care he sought to bring her to the United States. After repeated efforts her visa was denied. She passed away on January 19th, the same day that he finally received permission to bring her from Peru to the States. He would win the roses on May 6, 2006, but it was a bittersweet moment in knowing that his mother was no longer there to share his joy.

The Grass Is Greener

The two year old Barbaro had been entrusted to the care of trainer Michael Matz after he left the training grounds at John Stephenson's farm in Ocala. With the Stephensons, Barbaro was given time to mature at his own rate; there was no urgency to prepare the horse for juvenile sales. "It's all about giving a horse time to develop....Our program is geared toward the individual," said Stephenson. While with Jill and John Stephenson, Barbaro would be given extra outings to build stamina and endurance. By the spring of 2005 Barbaro was shipped to Michael Matz at Fair Hill Training Center in Elkton, Maryland. From there the wonderful story would begin to unfold.

Many of Michael Matz's training strategies have been labeled unconventional by some old school trainers and diehard horsemen. His core of beliefs addresses the importance of not over-training or exhausting the horse. As he related, "In 1976, I rode in the Olympics, and the whole team was fighting to see who would ride in the last spot." Matz then took his horse and repeatedly exercised him. Later he related,

When we finally got to the Olympics, I had no horse left. So I said from that day that whatever I do, whatever competition I go into, I want to make sure that I can be competitive, and that requires a fresh horse. I certainly want to come into a race with a horse that's fresh and hasn't raced too much. That was the whole plan from the beginning.

In all that Michael Matz did with Barbaro, he stood by his philosophical beliefs. When it came time to orchestrate a plan for Barbaro's racing schedule, there were many factors to consider. Both of his parents had done well on turf yet his dam LaVille Rouge had run equally as well on dirt. Many times the particular surface makes a difference to a horse's natural talent and these factors need to be considered by the trainer. On a turf, track horses are able to get a surer footing; a horse's foot tends to skid on dirt, and dirt surfaces place greater stress on muscles and joints. In exercising Barbaro, Matz felt that he was impressive on both turf and dirt, but time would tell.

The first race chosen for Barbaro, because of his late foaling on April 29th, was on the 4th of October at Delaware Park in Wilmington, Delaware. It was a mile long race on turf and "he broke his maiden" (won his first race) in an impressive fashion. All were more than pleased with his efforts. As Matz said, "One of the reasons that we designed this plan for Barbaro was because he started so late in the season. We wanted to put him in races that would not be too much for him." The next choice would be another turf race, six and one-half weeks later on November 19th in the Laurel Futurity at Laurel, Maryland. This time the distance was a little longer (by 1/16th mile) and the competition was more challenging.

In the Laurel Futurity Barbaro put on a dazzling performance for a 2-year old colt. Staying behind a 49-1 early leader, he kept poised until the far turn and then made his move. He won by a full 8 lengths beating Diabolical who had been his only real threat. At the conclusion of the race, it was decided that Barbaro would be wintering in Florida as a preparation for his all important 3-year old season. Matz suggested that further consideration may be given to Barbaro working on other surfaces. "I think we have to try him on the dirt….He really does have a lot of talent and I'd be tempted to see if it transfers from turf to dirt." Both owners supported Matz in his decision and had left the planning of Barbaro's course entirely in his hands.

The next race for Barbaro would be another turf race in Florida but with a different jockey. In the Tropical Park Derby on January 1st, Edgar Prado would be replacing Jose Caraballo. This race would be a test of sorts in three different ways: the length of the race would be slightly longer—1 1/8th, a different jockey would bring another assessment of the horse's ability, and the trainer and owners could ponder the turf v. dirt question one more time.

There is an old adage that suggests that what one does on New Year's Day sets a tone for the entire year. I'm certain that the Jacksons, Matzs and Prado would like to believe that, after Barbaro's triumph at Calder in the Tropical Park Derby. The victory was stunning and brought the colt to a record of 3-0, having trounced his competition in the three races by a total of over 20 lengths. His presence was so commanding that Prado added, "I could have been anywhere in the race that I wanted to be and still would have won. That's how good this horse is. He can be any kind of horse."

After the Tropical Park Derby a decision needed to be made. Barbaro had proved that he could dominate other horses on the turf, as his pedigree suggested. With the Kentucky Derby four months away, more of the horse's latent talents needed to be explored. "I would say you'd have to try the dirt now to see where he fits....He has enough class no matter which direction we try, but whether it's as much on the dirt we don't know," Matz added. The Jacksons were elated with his record regardless of where he ran. "We've been breeding for such a long time and it's great to have a horse of this caliber regardless of where Michael decides to run him," said Gretchen Jackson.

If Barbaro would take to the dirt, it would be at a time that provided the physical and mental rest that Michael Matz felt that the horse would need. One dirt race that was scheduled for February and looked somewhat inviting was the Holy Bull Stakes at Gulfstream Park.

A Three-Year Old Success Story

When the decision had been made to enter Barbaro in the Holy Bull Stakes on February 4th, a whole new round of questions began to surface about his ability on dirt. Michael Matz explained again that any horse with his background and talent needed to be given the opportunity. "We have taken our time with him. Physically, he was ready before, but mentally he had a lot of growing up to do. He's a big horse, well-mannered. He's a kind horse, nice to be around. He's a lot of horse, though, and you can't just have anyone ride him," said Matz. The early stages of a relationship with Edgar Prado had begun in the Tropical Derby, and Matz hoped for that consistency to exist for Barbaro if he were headed to Churchill Downs in early May.

In preparation for the Holy Bull Stakes, Matz continued with his plan of keeping the horse tuned-up without tiring him out with rigorous and frequent workouts. The day of the race offered an even greater challenge than plain old dirt; the track was as sloppy as it could be after a whole day of rain at Gulfstream. In his turf races, Barbaro had had the excellent footing and incredible speed which were needed to pull the victory out of the slop. It was not a classical introduction to a different surface, but the colt weathered the storm nonetheless. His margin of victory was three-quarters of a length. "I was happy with his performance," remarked Prado. "He proved today that he could go either way." Concerning Barbaro's next venue, Matz announced that Barbaro would now pursue a campaign on the dirt. "Since we're here in Florida, I suppose we'll look at either the Fountain of Youth Stakes or the Florida Derby."

The Florida Derby would be Matz's choice for Barbaro's final prep race for the Kentucky Derby. After an eight week lay-off, the naysayers were back with more questions and challenges for Matz. This would be the very first Grade I stakes race for Barbaro, his first experience on a dry, fast dirt track and a different group of three-year olds. Formerly held in the middle of March, the Florida Derby would not be attracting the same level of hard-core competition that it had in days gone by. Most trainers had their eyes set on Derby prep races that were closer to May 5th. A five-week layoff was too much time, and another race could not comfortably be squeezed in between April 1st and May 5th. To complicate all of the firsts for Barbaro was the less-than-pleasant choice of post position 10 in a field of eleven. Would it take too much out of him to break properly and get to the lead without any problems?

In the morning line Barbaro was the 8-5 favorite and undoubtedly the horse to beat. The purse of $1 million dollars was on the table, but many people still questioned Barbaro's ability to handle the track and the difficult post. Among the competition trainers, Nick Zito felt, "Barbaro is a good horse, but this is a huge step, and we'll see if he really handles a fast track like he does the turf or slop. There certainly are some questions he still needs to answer." About the post position, Matz felt, "Naturally I'd like to be closer to the inside, but it shouldn't be a problem. It's a short run to the first turn, but he should be able to put himself in a good spot right behind Sharp Humor, who figures to set the pace."

The race proved to be very much of a fast duel between Barbaro and a very commanding Sharp Humor with Barbaro prevailing at the rail by a half-length. Michael Matz's plan of 8 week's rest had received some redemption although the media was now focusing on the 5 week's rest before the Kentucky Derby. This unorthodox five week's lay-off had not been done with positive results for fifty years since Needles won the Derby. The response of Michael Matz was, "It's about time. Don't you think?"

The Derby Challenge

As the first Saturday in May was rapidly approaching, Michael Matz kept with his training plan. Exercise rider Peter Brette, who had ridden Barbaro since his arrival at Fairhill, spent everyday with Barbaro and totally concurred with Matz's assessment. Marveling at Barbaro's arsenal of power, Brette commented,

The first time I sat on him it was like riding a 3-year-old. I told Michael before his first start this was the best horse I've ever been on. He was pretty backward and immature...but he had a great big stride and a beautiful way of moving....He's gotten to a stage now where there is always another gear. That's what makes him special. No one knows how good he really is, because we've never gotten to the bottom of him. But we may get to the bottom of him on Derby Day.

Both men knew that they had found a once-in-a-lifetime horse. What remained was the chance to show that to the rest of the world.

Many trainers cringe at the media circus that the Kentucky Derby can create. There is so much hoopla for the entire week, that some stay away as long as they can. Michael Matz had Barbaro flown from Florida to the Keeneland Racetrack in Lexington, which would remain home base for a large part of the time before the Derby. The grade I and grade II stakes-winning horses coming into the race would undoubtedly be considered favorites, and deserving of more than their share of media attention. As expected, Michael Matz would be listening to replays of significant events in his life: the United Flight 232 rescue, his three Olympic performances, his Silver Medal at the Atlanta Olympics and his flag-carrying in the Closing Ceremonies. Being one who does not relish media, Matz would have to "grin-and-bear-it" all week long. The authorities at Churchill Downs had arranged for the Roth siblings, now 26, 29 and 31, to come to the Derby as their guests. It was a great human interest story that would be discussed throughout the week. Additional attention would be focused on the Jacksons since their two horses were the only undefeated horses in the Derby, and their Philadelphia connections came on the heels of Smarty Jones and Afleet Alex. In another human interest way, Edgar Prado's tragic loss of his mother would be shared as would her inability to get to the States for timely and necessary medical attention. All of these little pieces would keep the media blitz alive and well for hours and hours. So many stories were surrounding one horse, but there were 19 other horses in the race.

Post positions were drawn in the middle of the week and Barbaro would be number 8. This number would put him in the thick of things, but experienced jockeys are more familiar with maneuvering around in a field of 20 horses. It would be Prado's role to place himself behind a speedball, like Lawyer Ron, Sharp Humor or Brother Derek, to avoid being wedged in the middle. Another option was to follow the horses that break quickly, like Sinister Minister or Sweetnorthernsaint. All-in-all it promised to be a very fast race. Those in the lead early could be spent; while others could be left behind. None of these horses had ever run a 1-1/4 mile race, so all were being asked to do something completely new. Only time would tell.

The crowd assembling at Churchill Downs for the 132nd Kentucky Derby would be one of the largest on record, 157,536, with some stylish (and some crazy)hats and traditional mint juleps everywhere. The strains of Stephen Foster's "Old Kentucky Home," would follow the call to post and then the drama would begin. Few could stand on this "holy ground" without feeling an emotional thrill; after all, it is the "greatest two minutes in sports."

At six-fifteen Eastern Time the gates sprang open and the race began. Everyone gasped as Barbaro stumbled out of the gate, but recovered just as quickly and fell behind the early leaders, Keyed Entry, Sinister Minister, Sharp Humor and Showing Up. The momentum continued with leaders changing places as Barbaro cruised at a comfortable pace. After three-quarters in a strong 1:10.88 the field bunched up, but Barbaro kept his place. In no time he took off and for the rest it was going to be all about second money. Barbaro was in the clear with nothing more than a ride home from Prado. He kept increasing his lead, and drew away from the others for a victory in 2:01.36. His final quarter a :24.34 was one of the fastest in Derby history, and his margin was 6 1/2 lengths, the best in sixty years since Assault in 1946. At the wire, all that could be heard was the sportscaster screaming, "It's all Barbaro! It's all Barbaro!"

As Barbaro progressed to the Winner's Circle, it was something special for Team Barbaro. It was a first-time Derby win for the owners, the trainer and the jockey—a special kind of Trifecta. It was more than any one of them could have hoped for in a million years.

For the victory of Barbaro to be linked to Assault touched a special spot in D. D. Matz's heart, for she is the granddaughter of Robert Kleburg of King

Ranch in Texas. It was under the silks of King Ranch in 1946 that Assault had won his astonishing Triple Crown. Another first for the Matzs' was the five week lay-off that had the more conservative trainers in a tizzy. As Steve Haskin in his *Blood-Horse* article so aptly said,

> If there was a louder noise on this day, it was the sound of a trainer's guide on how to prepare a horse for the Kentucky Derby being ripped to shreds. By saddling Barbaro to win the Derby off a five-week layoff, something that hadn't been accomplished in half a century, and preparing the horse with only one race in 13 weeks leading up to the Derby, Matz has rewritten the bible for most trainers on their journey to Churchill Downs.

The media reacted to the victory by acting somewhat sheepish around Matz. He had been tortured for his plan, but he was too much of a gentleman to call them on it. His response was, "What can I say? Everybody saw it....He never missed anything, and we never wavered from our plans. It looks like we made the right plan." For the Jacksons it was a thrilling time, "It was probably one of the happiest moments of my life; it's exhilarating; it's the best," recalled Gretchen Jackson. For Edgar Prado it was vindication for all of those Derbies without a win. He completed his own personal Triple Crown for his mother, Cenaida.

From this point on, the pace would hasten. The Preakness Stakes was only two weeks away and then the Belmont Stakes. The ultimate prize for the Triple Crown was more than just three different races. It challenged the horse from the standpoint of time for preparation, the amount of travel and the length of races. In days gone by some of the iron horses of the '40s wouldn't have batted an eye at the rigorous pace. The great Citation won the Triple Crown, which at the time had the races spaced differently. He won the Derby and then two weeks later, triumphed at Pimlico. In 1948, there were four weeks between the Preakness and the Belmont, so Ben Jones chose to have Citation run in the New Jersey Stakes, later to be called derby, on May 29th to keep him fit. In today's training manual that would have been unheard of, but in the past the horses were conditioned differently and some believe they had greater stamina. Unfortunately in today's thoroughbreds, we look for everything. As Dan Rosenberg, President of Three Chimneys Farm, so aptly suggested, "There is commercially more of an emphasis on speed. Just like a pickup truck is a lot more durable than a Maserati, there is an inherent incompatibility between speed and durability." This may be the reason that many of our more recent champions don't "stick around" very long; we are asking for more than they may be able to give.

In the two weeks between the Kentucky Derby and the Preakness, Barbaro was taken back to Fair Hill Training Center, not too far from the Pennsylvania border, where Michael Matz did most of his training in the spring, summer and fall. During this time Barbaro would be able to relax in the paddock and be a normal horse for a while. At the last possible minute he would be driven over to Pimlico Race Course, in Baltimore, Maryland.

History Stands Still

The title of the "Triple Crown" had been a brainstorm of the veteran Daily Racing Form writer, Charlie Hatton. In 1930, Hatton had been writing about the exploits that year of Gallant Fox. The horse had taken the Kentucky Derby, the Preakness Stakes and the Belmont Stakes, and according to Hatton, he was deserving of a triple crown. For an owner, it would represent a lot of money and prestige. For the horse achieving it, there would be no doubt about his or her talent and ability as an equine athlete. Over the course of the last century only eleven horses have made the mark, for it can be a grueling task. The three races of different lengths span a five- week period, at three different racing venues, in three different states.

In recent years, a limited number of trainers have attempted entrance into all three Triple Crown races with the same horse unless the horse is in contention for the coveted award. Many horses have won two of the jewels. Within the last ten years, seven contenders were within one victory of the crown. The most tragic loss of recent memory was Smarty Jones's bid at Belmont in 2004. He led the field during the entire race, only to lose in the last three seconds by one length to Birdstone. For Smarty (2004) and Afleet Alex (2005), the Belmont Stakes brought career-ending injuries.

At the age of three, a thoroughbred's bones are still growing and developing. Many countries do not race their young athletes at two, because they perceive the long- term effects could be detrimental to their animals. Most trainers are very vigilant to any subtle problems with their young horses and frequently scratch them from a race should there be a health-related concern. Any trainer or owner will concede that on any day and at any given moment, a horse can encounter a problem with the track and be seriously injured. The horse's delicate and narrow legs support over one thousand pounds, and at high speeds almost anything can happen. A good jockey is an invaluable resource, for many times he/she senses if a horse isn't feeling well or has issues walking or cantering. Track veterinarians, too, are trained to examine any horse prior to a race if they should notice anything unusual in the horse's gait or behavior. Careful attention is paid to every horse in the paddock area, prior to any given race.

As Barbaro was resting up for the Preakness, Michael Matz chose to use his own training facility at Fair Hill in Maryland. The plan would continue in a very methodical fashion without stressing or tiring the horse. Jockeys and trainers alike marveled at Barbaro's burst of speed at the Derby without even breaking a sweat. By design, the Preakness is a shorter race than the Derby-1/8 of a mile less. Ordinarily, too, the field of horses is fewer. Some trainers pass on the Preakness and opt for the Belmont, because it is thought to be the greatest test at 1-1/2 miles and therefore the greatest victory. Few are up to its demands for both speed and stamina.

On the day before the Preakness Stakes, Barbaro arrived at Pimlico Race Course to a hero's welcome. The pace had been somewhat relaxed and the horse was more than ready for the race. It had been a media-driven two weeks, but Barbaro had gotten rest and exercise in a very comfortable environment—his own bed! In a post position of six, Prado could make good choices early on and set Barbaro at a nice pace from the start.

In the paddock area, Barbaro seemed feisty. Some horses can be resistant to being saddled and once it's an accomplished fact, they're fine. During warm-ups with Prado, he was responsive and fit. The horses and their riders would take their places to strains of "Maryland, My Maryland," sung by the midshipmen from the Naval Academy in Annapolis. When all were posed and ready, Barbaro sprang his gate early with a firm push and took off. He would be intercepted by an out-rider, who would steer him back to circumvent the starting gate. A false start is never taken lightly by jockeys or trainers, and many times considered a bad omen. It is thought that it may upset the horse's timing and cause a loss of momentum the second time. Before returning to post position, Barbaro was carefully examined by both the Pimlico track vet and the Maryland Racing Association vet. He was deemed to be fit, and the protocols continued.

With a clang of the bell, the doors sprang open, and the horses were off. At one point in the early strides they seemed to be colliding, but just as quickly the pack appeared to settle into a cadence. Within 100 yards of the gate, Edgar Prado heard a snap as Barbaro broke his pastern bone. Considering the horse's power and momentum, it took all of Prado's strength to pull him up, but not before he had continued running and caused further damage to his right rear leg. As the horse stood relatively still, everyone could see the agony of the moment.

Trainers would applaud Prado's efforts, which saved the horse from the type of injury that the great filly Ruffian had suffered by grinding her leg into the gravel and dirt during the Great Match Race of 1975. For Barbaro, the extra fifty yards of running had broken additional bones, which would later complicate the injury. At that instant, too, there was the horrible realization by Barbaro that he could not stand on all four legs. He stood and froze; he balanced on three legs.

On national television, an audience of millions gasped in horror as Barbaro lifted his helpless limb with the ankle dangling attached only by a few loose tendons. A traumatized Edgar Prado held the horse in place, while he rested all of his weight against the frightened animal to help him keep his balance on three legs. The Jacksons, Matzs and veterinarians charged across the track to the injured horse, while a stunned crowd at Pimlico went silent. At one point a large blue screen was lifted on to the track should it be necessary to euthanize Barbaro based on the extent of his injuries. In many cases this is a positive alternative, instead of allowing an animal to struggle in agony with an injury that realistically cannot be treated. Horses live and die on their feet, and must have quality of life and equal distribution of those 1000 plus pounds.

At the sight of the screen, the frantic crowd began screaming, "No! No! Don't put Barbaro down!" Many people were in tears, parents were comforting their children and some were lost in their own thoughts, as the drama unfolded before them. As the race continued, some made feeble attempts to watch the other horses, but the real contest would belong to Barbaro and his caregivers. Within minutes, the equine ambulance was on the track surface and preparations were being made to stabilize the joint and to load Barbaro on to the vehicle. A Kimsey splint was placed on the right hind leg, and Michael Matz held the door open as Barbaro was led on to the ambulance. As the horse moved forward on to the vehicle, a round of applause could be heard from Barbaro's public. With that the ambulance sped away. Destination: New Bolton Center of the Hospital of the University of Pennsylvania, Kennett Square, Pennsylvania.

"Good to the Bone"

In the June 10th, 2007 issue of the *Blood-Horse*, Terry Conway referred to Dr. Dean Richardson as "good to the bone." As an equine orthopedic surgeon of long-standing, nothing could be closer to the truth. Those who know Richardson well will tell you that he wrote the book, literally and figuratively, on how to repair many equine fractures. In the past he had treated many of Gretchen and Roy Jacksons' horses very successfully, and this was the single reassuring and comforting thought for Barbaro's connections as the ambulance made its way to New Bolton Center.

For Dean Richardson, however, veterinary medicine had not been on his personally-prepared career list as he arrived at Dartmouth University at the tender age of sixteen. As the son of a Navy Captain, whose specialty had been internal medicine, Dean's earliest aspirations revolved around the theatre and acting. The family had traveled extensively here and abroad as part of the career-oriented Navy regimen. With a background as diversified as this, the talented student had many avenues open to him. Upon his arrival at Dartmouth, however, Richardson took a routine physical education/horseback-riding course and never looked back.

While attending college, he chose to surround himself with horse-related activities. As his devotion and respect for all things equine grew, he took realistic stock of his theatrical options and chose to pursue a doctoral degree in veterinary medicine at Ohio State University. After the completion of this degree, he made his way to New Bolton Center, where he has remained for the last twenty-eight years.

When he first arrived at this large animal facility for the University of Pennsylvania Veterinary School, he served as an intern with Dr. Mitch Leitch. Years later she would remark of Richardson's ability to integrate large amounts of information and envision possibilities that eluded others. She described his surgery techniques as, "Magical." It is not unusual for him to work on cases that ordinarily would not yield positive outcomes. He is a perfectionist who may be intimidating to others. Leitsch added, "He is a powerful intellectual force."

For the veterinary surgeons, who choose to work within the parameters of a teaching hospital, their practice is both challenging and changing. At New Bolton Center, the newest research trends must be in the forefront, as well as their mentoring of the equine surgeons of the future. It is not the least bit unusual for them to be called upon to assist their colleagues in the field with difficult procedures. Such was the case on Preakness Saturday, May 20th, 2006.

At this time, Dr. Richardson was completing a couple of challenging surgeries with friend, Dr. Byron Reid in Loxahatchee, Florida. Both surgeons had taken a break to watch the Preakness, so Richardson's view of the misstep was timely and telling. Even a distance of 1,200 miles and a six-inch television screen could not obscure the horse's agony and the limb's distortion. As his cell phone began to ring off the hook, Richardson prepared for the inevitable -Barbaro would be his patient upon his return to Philadelphia.

While still in Florida, Dr. Richardson would receive Barbaro's digital X-rays through email in anticipation of surgery. The Jacksons had offered a private plane to bring the surgeon home sooner, but Richardson perceived it as an unnecessary expense. "I knew I wasn't going to do surgery in the next 12 hours or so. It's not generally a good idea to take a fit horse that just broke down on the racetrack and is extremely stressed, right into extensive surgery. He needed time to quiet down."

Over the years, veterinary medicine has made wonderful strides in the timing and extent to which animals' injuries may be successfully managed. What may have been considered impossible and cost-prohibitive twenty years ago, has become a routine procedure due to the use of technology and the wonders of research. When Ruffian was treated for her fractured leg in 1975, no thought was given to postponing the surgery. She went into the operation in a highly excited and agitated state, and twice was resuscitated during the procedure due to her systems reeling out of control. In Barbaro's case, he would be the recipient of the wisdom and experience gleaned from her loss.

Prior to leaving Pimlico, Barbaro's limb had been placed in a Kimsey splint. This enabled the horse to be taken to his stall for an examination and X-rays. As Dr. Dan Dreyfuss explained, "The Kimsey is the aluminum splint that essentially has a cup that the hoof goes into. There is a rigid strut that goes up the front of the leg and Velcro straps that you can wrap around to hold it in place." At this point the horse would have been given tranquillizers and non-steroidal anti-inflammatory medication. An additional series of bandages would be applied, and intravenous antibiotics would be administered before placing Barbaro back into the equine ambulance for the one and one-half hour trip to Kennett Square.

As Barbaro's equine ambulance sped toward New Bolton Center, the highways and overpasses were lined with fans bearing signs with well wishes. Prior to the horse's arrival, the gate and fence at the hospital were adorned with cards and gifts, as part of an unprecedented outpouring of love and care from the American public. The operators at the hospital and the hits on the New Bolton Center website would give further testimony to the public's stake in Barbaro's horrific injury and impending surgery. Millions of Americans were onboard for the long haul, and they were hoping against hope that Barbaro would beat the odds.

When Barbaro arrived at New Bolton Center in a media storm, he would be placed in the care of Dr. Barbara Dallup, an emergency clinician. She would report to the media the following day, "We stabilized him overnight. He has been extremely brave and well-behaved in this situation. He has been very comfortable and has done quite well so far." This team of intensive care doctors would monitor Barbaro and keep the horse as comfortable as possible in anticipation of Dr. Richardson's arrival. The surgery was scheduled for the early afternoon of May 21st.

Prior to the surgery, Dr. Richardson conducted a news conference with the media who had camped out since the previous evening. His remarks to the reporters were simple yet "cut to the chase." The injuries which Barbaro had sustained were a condylar fracture of the cannon bone, a shattered first phalanx (more than 20 pieces), a fractured sesamoid and a dislocated fetlock joint. "We do not see this severe of an injury very frequently because of the fact that most horses that suffer this severe of an injury are typically put down on the racetrack. It's about as bad as it can be. It is very unusual to see these three catastrophic injuries all piled into one leg." When asked when the surgery would commence, the reply was, "When you stop asking me questions."

The surgery performed on Barbaro would take a full six hours to complete. Assisting Richardson were several New Bolton Center residents: Dr. Liberty Gutman, Dr. Steve Zedler, Dr. David Levine and anesthesiologist Dr. Ben Driessen. With careful monitoring of the horse's vital signs, the task demanded the reassembling of all of the shattered bones. In some instances, bones had been pulverized and no longer fit together well. The closest visual analogy would be a bag of ice with its many irregular pieces. These were reconfigured with titanium screws, or implants, allowing the broken fragments to be held together. A single LCP, locking compression plate, was added within the leg and at least 27 titanium screws before the operation was completed. Another critical area surrounded the blood supply within the horse's leg. Richardson reported, "One of the concerns that we did have was whether or not he had a reasonably good blood supply to the distal limb…When we did the procedure, we had good blood supply throughout, so I was happy with that."

When the surgery was completed, special attention was given to bringing Barbaro successfully out of the anesthesia. In 1975, when Ruffian's operation was over, she was placed on a large mat in a padded stall. As she awakened, she became disoriented and continued to run as if she were still racing. Her limbs collided and smashed each other, leaving the veterinarians no other alternative but euthanasia. In Barbaro's case, the pool recovery system was employed which allows the horse to awaken with an inability to further injure itself. While being suspended in a sling, the horse is lowered into a large rubber raft with four sleeves permitting the horse's legs to be submerged in the water. The temperature of the water is very warm (97degrees) and this has a positive effect on the animal. As Richardson explained,

> The horse's legs are immersed down in the water, but it [the horse] stays dry because it is inside this raft. Then the horse wakes up completely from the anesthesia. The idea is that if the horse struggles, it cannot hurt itself because it's struggling only against the resistance of the water. The water is very, very toasty and warm, and the horses like it....But eventually, they wake up, and they want to get out. Then we put a blindfold on them, lift them up, and take them to a stall, and set them down on their feet.

At the conclusion of a procedure of this nature, it is imperative that the horse remain standing. Barbaro did better than that for he jumped around several times. This did not excite Richardson who said, "He didn't really hurt anything, and that's all that really matters. He walked on the leg immediately, and that's what you're looking for. He was standing completely on his own, and ...practically jogged back to his stall."

The World Holds Its Breath

When Barbaro's operation was completed, the media covered every aspect of the surgery and recuperation. This horse had become a victim in a large and very public arena, and every aspect related to his care had become a matter of national interest. There were literally thousands of email "get well" wishes sent through the University of Pennsylvania website, hundreds of baskets of flowers delivered to New Bolton, and more carrots and apples donated than any horse could eat in a lifetime. Many of the locals kept vigil at the entrances, and fans traveled long distances to hang banners and cards on the hospital gates and fences.. The hourly news broadcasts carried pertinent updates as well as footage from both the Derby and Preakness. The Jacksons, Dr. Dean Richardson and Michael Matz were very accommodating to the press, and frequent news conferences were held to educate the public on the technical nuances of equine medicine.

On the day after the surgery, all of Barbaro's health reports were glowing. All of the basic vital signs were good and Barbaro looked like a pain-free and happy horse. In a very crowded news conference, Richardson cautioned the public not to become overly confident as Barbaro's survival was still a "coin toss," and would be for many months. In a surgery as complicated as Barbaro's had been, there were many things that could go wrong. The risk of infection was always a real possibility, as well as issues related to the horse's distribution of his weight equally on all four limbs. When questioned on these concerns, Richardson said, "As long as he's comfortable, this is less likely to occur." Other questions addressed Barbaro's ability to breed as a stallion with the nature of his injury. Before the assembled audience and national TV, Richardson made it quite clear that the attempts to save the horse's life were just that. He stated,

> I made a point about how the optimal outcome for the horse is that he be salvaged for breeding. And some people are taking that the wrong way. I want everyone to understand that if this horse were a gelding, these owners would have definitely done everything to save this horse's life. I know the Jacksons a long time. This horse could have no reproductive value, and they would have saved this horse's life.

What everyone wanted for Barbaro at this point, in Gretchen Jackson's words, "would be to live a good quality life." This was the end to which everyone was working.

In the first ten days after surgery, Barbaro's condition could not have been better. On May 30th, Dr. Richardson noted, "He's actually done far better than we could have ever hoped for, so far. He's perfectly comfortable and all of his vital signs are normal. His blood work is good, and basically, at this moment, he could not look any better in terms of his medical condition. His prognosis is much better than it was, but he still has a long way to go." The "long way to go" phrase would follow Barbaro for many weeks and months. Dr. Richardson added, "When we change his cast will literally be a day-by-day decision. Right now, this horse is walking so well on his limb, he willingly rests his left hind, and he's very active walking around his stall." In an attempt to reduce the threat of laminitis in the left hind leg, a specially-designed horseshoe was applied to the foot during surgery. This shoe would provide the much-needed support, as well as compensate for the additional length of the cast on the right hind leg. The horse would remain in the Intensive Care unit at New Bolton Center for many weeks and receive around the clock care from the team of doctors and nurses.

The month of June brought the Belmont Stakes on June 10th and Barbaro made an appearance on national television from his stall at New Bolton. This was very far removed from what the fans had originally envisioned for him on this day, but Barbaro did get an up-close-and- personal look at Jazil's victory at Belmont from his own personal TV. Barbaro's medical team believed that the colt was progressing nicely, "He is doing extremely well, and has been especially frisky, displaying interest in nearby mares that are also at the hospital." On the 13th of the month, Dr. Richardson did something that was thought to be dramatic-he changed Barbaro's cast. New radiographs were taken and the condition of the leg was described as, "Excellent!" Later on the 20th, he assessed Barbaro's condition once again, "He's a lively, bright, happy horse. If you asked me a month ago, I would have gladly accepted where we are today." Also, within the month, a $13.5 million dollar gift from the state of Pennsylvania was presented in his name for new medical facilities, which would enable New Bolton to continue as a world class facility.

During the first week of July, some of Barbaro's vital signs changed which raised a caution flag. His elevated body temperature and general uncomfortable state, caused Dr. Richardson and his staff to examine the cast and the injured leg. Under general anesthesia, the cast was changed and three new screws inserted. Two days later when the horse appeared to be experiencing discomfort, the cast was changed once more and the horse was treated for a small abscess on the sole of his left hind foot. The primary fracture appeared to be healing well, but the shattered pastern joint continued to be more of a concern. The joint was stabilized with a new bone graft and fresh implants. On July 8th, for the third time in one week, Barbaro was placed under anesthesia to replace the plate and screws surrounding his fracture. The colt was treated for a high fever and infection as complications of his initial injury. Dr. Richardson released a statement, through New Bolton Center, that the situation was "potentially serious," and in an interview on TV, he spoke of "tough days ahead."

On the evening of July 12th, Dr. Richardson met with the Jacksons and Michael Matz to discuss Barbaro's prognosis. The one complication that had been dreaded had now become a reality—laminitis. Richardson described Barbaro's laminitis in terms of "it's as bad as it gets." The laminae are tiny strands which connect the horse's bottom bone (the coffin bone) to its hoof. When they become inflamed, they separate and lose their grip on the inside of the hoof. It became necessary for Dr. Richardson to remove 80% of the horse's left rear hoof wall. For any horse, this is a grim prognosis and coupled with the severe injuries to the right hind leg from the Preakness, Barbaro's condition was very, very serious.

During the first days of July, there had been numerous complications with the injured right leg, which caused the horse to place additional weight on the left hind leg. It is this uneven distribution which causes the highly painful and life-threatening disease of laminitis. The great Secretariat lost his life with this disease, and few options exist for animals that must remain erect and standing.

Horses cannot spend large periods of time lying down, as this positioning compromises their vascular and digestive systems. It was imperative that Barbaro could stand comfortably and evenly on all four legs. From the very beginning of his treatment, the Jacksons, Dr. Richardson and Michael Matz had agreed that this scenario was the goal and anything less would be deemed unacceptable as far as allowing Barbaro's life to continue.

On the 17th of July, Barbaro's condition had remained stable for four straight days, but his long-term prognosis was still uncertain. The roller coaster ride had kept the newscasters on their toes, and Barbaro's fans could not obtain frequent enough updates to ease their troubled minds. Several of the Barbaro faithful had set up websites for those who wished to be informed regularly of the colt's progress. One such site was timwoolleyracing.com, which was updated several times daily through the Fairhill Training Center in Maryland. Michael Matz would visit with Barbaro and pertinent details would be passed on to webmaster Alex Brown. It was not the least bit unusual for the site to receive 25,000 hits per day with at least 1,500 personal messages left. As the colt's progress remained unremarkable, many of the TV stations ceased carrying daily updates and these websites fulfilled a real need in communication.

By the beginning of August, Barbaro had been enjoying a number of good days. Dr. Richardson's reports included a lot more of what everyone was hoping and praying to hear. "Barbaro's condition continues to be stable…the left hind hoof is slowly showing evidence of regrowth…the original fractures have apparently healed well…his left hind hoof continues to show signs of regrowth and looks healthy…and, Barbaro is doing well on both hind limbs." The horse was doing well enough to graze outside the clinic. Dr. Richardson felt that Barbaro was more than ready for a change in scenery, and the fresh air and sunshine would be added benefits as he picked his own grass. Mr. and Mrs. Jackson were making daily trips from home with fresh grass and other treats. Things were generally looking up from the grim prognosis of July, but there were many more things that needed to improve for Barbaro to be "out of the woods."

Many very positive things happened for Barbaro during the month of September. His surgeon, Dr. Richardson felt that the colt would soon have his cast removed, "The pastern joint looks completely fused, and there is only a small area in the long pastern bone that has a little farther to go before we take him out of the cast completely." During the week of September 18th good things continued to happen. "He had an excellent week," reported Dr. Richardson. "We replaced the boot on his left hind foot with a bandage because the hoof is doing well….He is enjoying his daily excursions outside to graze, and his appetite is excellent."

Into the month of October, Barbaro continued to improve. The right hind leg injuries were almost entirely healed, but the laminitic left hind hoof continued to grow at a very slow rate. His surgeon, Dr. Richardson believed that it could take as long as six months to a year to regrow the 80% of the hoof wall that had been surgically removed in July. The fans had placed banners stating, "Grow, Hoof, Grow," on the New Bolton Center fences reminding all who passed by that this was still very much an area of concern for the horse's survival. Dr. Richardson's report of the week of October 24, 2006 said it best, "The hoof is growing slowly and not uniformly, so it has a long way to go before it is acceptably strong and functional. The foot will require meticulous care for a long time and setbacks here and there are probable."

On the 6th of November, Barbaro had the cast removed from his lower right hind leg and enjoyed a perfect pool recovery after anesthesia. One of the greatest pieces of news was that Barbaro walked back to his stall after the procedure and used all of his legs well as he walked. The left hind foot still represented a challenge, but for all intent and purposes the horse appeared to be halfway home. For Barbaro's connections, good things were also happening. Team Barbaro was the recipient of the Jim "Sunny Jim" Fitzsimmons Award, for a person or group typifying the spirit of racing. As Mr. Jackson accepted the award, he thanked everyone who had assisted Barbaro in any way. He also addressed the laminitis topic and the antislaughter bill as areas which would require attention and support in the future.

The month of December ushered in a flurry of excitement that Barbaro might be moved to a new home in the very near future. With this news flash came a strong ray of hope for Barbaro's fans, who were constantly worried about the horse's long-term prognosis. The move would be for the horse's physical well-being. Barbaro should continue to enjoy the sun and fresh air which a warmer climate could provide. From the standpoint of his recuperating hind legs, the general public had not lost sight of Dr. Richardson's initial and haunting prognosis for Barbaro-"a coin toss-a 50/50 chance for survival."

On December 19th, Dr. Scott Morrison, from Rood and Riddle Equine Hospital in Lexington, examined Barbaro's left hind foot, performed some work and made some recommendations. The medical staff reexamined the timetable at this moment concerning Barbaro's discharge from the hospital. His comfort on both hind limbs was good and his overall condition was excellent." This was a Christmas present of sorts for many of his fans.

In 2006, Barbaro and his connections had ushered in the New Year with a convincing victory at the Tropical Park Derby at Calder, with Edgar Prado aboard for the first time. What a difference a year makes, as the Kentucky Derby dazzler was trying to win the biggest challenge of his career as a patient at New Bolton Center. On January 2nd, Dr. Richardson assessed that the colt's injured right hind leg was getting stronger, and he believed the horse eventually capable of living a comfortable and happy life.

One week later, Barbaro was experiencing some discomfort in his left hind foot and more separation was located in the hoof. At that time a previously applied cast was removed. On the 13th, another section of the laminitic-stricken left hind foot was discovered and removed by Dr. Richardson and a cast was placed on the right hind foot for support. On the 18th Barbaro was listed as improving. By the 24th, Dr. Richardson and his staff were pleased with their patient's progress, and a new cast was placed on the left hind leg. Dr. Scott Morrison had prepared a custom-made plastic and steel brace for the right hind leg, as a means of additional support. Within two days (January 26th) the brace had caused significant discomfort for the horse in his right hind leg, a deep abscess was detected and the cast was removed. The leg that had been the supportive limb throughout the entire laminitis ordeal was now in very serious condition. Dr. Richardson operated on Barbaro on the 27th to place steel pins as an external fixator on the ailing right leg to eliminate any additional weight bearing. The procedure is risky in so far as it puts a large measure of strain on the newly healed bones. For the first time, Barbaro had lost the ability to stand and lie down with ease; there was no position in which the horse could be comfortable.

On the morning of January 29th, 2007, the country lost a great hero. The timwoolleyracing.com entry 1403 was as follows: "Barbaro was euthanized at 10:30 am....Mr. and Mrs. Jackson and Dr. Dean Richardson were all in attendance."

Barbaro's sire, Dynaformer (right) stands (as a breeding Stallion) at Three Chimneys Farm in Midway, Kentucky. A full brother of Barbaro, Nicanor (immediately below), has begun his training in Ocala, Florida.

Barbaro's dam, LaVille Rouge is a broodmare at Mill Ridge Farm. She resides there with her unnamed foal (born April 2007). She was bred back to Dynaformer in May 2007; a new foal is expected in Spring 2008.

Barbaro was trained by
Michael Matz at the
Fair Hill Training Center
in Elkton, Maryland.
Michael Matz joins Barbaro
and his exercise rider,
Peter Brette, for a workout
between the 2006 Kentucky
Derby and the Preakness
Stakes.

Barbaro's stunning performance in the 2006 Kentucky Derby is remembered by all. His victory margin was the greatest in sixty years. Shown are the paddock at Churchill Downs and the winner's mannequin horse and rider that are enshrined in the owner's silks for one year in the Kentucky Derby Museum.

Barbaro spent eight months and eight days at Widener New Bolton Center of the University of Pennsylvania's School of Veterinary Medicine, as he recuperated from the fractures in his right hind leg. The fences there were constantly adorned with posters, get well messages and other gifts. Shown in the background is the historical farmhouse on the facility's campus.

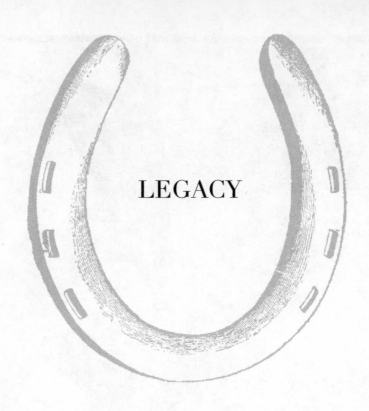

LEGACY

"The greatness of a nation and its moral progress can be judged by the way its animals are treated." - Mahatma Gandhi

Charismatic Horses

In the course of America's history, there have been moments of triumph and conquest, and there have been other moments of disappointment and depression. During the '70s, the nation was grappling with a frustrating war, a struggling economy, warring political factions and mounting discontent. The masses needed a distraction, something to cheer for, something to get excited about, something to dispel the doldrums in which America found itself.

It was on to this stage that Ruffian made her appearance, as an elegant black flash of brilliance. The anointing of a white star on her forehead served as a suggestion of the greatness that was to come. She would hold America hostage to her wiles for not too much more than the blink of an eye. In her ten races and ten victories, she did not spend more than fifteen actual minutes on a racetrack, but she captured the fancy of a large segment of the American public. She won the filly Triple Crown in astounding fashion, set or equaled track records and decimated her competition. She was the special jewel in the '70s Triple Crown setting, flanked by Secretariat, Seattle Slew and Affirmed, but had no difficulty standing on her own four feet and making her own statement.

Ruffian brought people into the world of racing who previously had nothing more than a casual interest. Those who watched her will never forget her. Those who missed that golden moment in time are relegated to books and racing DVDs. In the annals of thoroughbred racing, she will always be the measuring rod for all fillies and many colts. She did everything well, but the fates were not on her side, as she smashed her fragile ankle into the starting gate in an ill-conceived match race. The only blessing, if you could actually call it that, was the short window of her suffering—eight hours.

Every racetrack breakdown revives her memory, and every exciting young filly star will be compelled to stand in her shadow. The *Blood-Horse* ranked Ruffian 35th in a list of the top 100 Thoroughbreds of all time. When *Sports Illustrated* listed the Top 100 Female Athletes of the Century, Ruffian was the only non-human honoree. She is one of the all-time greats.

At the time of her death, there were many outpourings of love and devotion by the American public. One of the most poignant came from the children of Lexington, Kentucky. In a *Daily Racing Form* article of December 1976, Logan Bailey outlined how Ruffian's memory touched a group of young children, newbie riders, from 4H clubs and the like, who collected nickels to erect a granite monument in her honor. With the help of parents and community leaders, a large stone was placed in Masterson Station Park. The inscription, written by Cary Robertson, Jr., reads as follows:

This memorial erected in memory of RUFFIAN–We were young when she died, too young to number her with the greats of other eras. Yet to love, grace and perfection is ours because we are human and none felt her loss more painfully than we. The Children of Lexington

The monument is still in place today. For those who visit the park, the main thoroughfare is called Ruffian Way.

Everyday at Claiborne Farm in Paris, Kentucky, tours are conducted. One of the tour guides and stallion staff, Tony Battaglia shares the wonderful exploits of Ruffian, Secretariat and the other stars of Claiborne Farm Their history is rich–reaching back to include six of eleven Triple Crown winners, sixty-two Triple Crown race winners and twenty-three Breeders' Cup winners as offspring of their breeding program. In his tour, Tony will speak of Ruffian as the greatest filly ever and her accomplishments are shared with another generation of horse lovers.

Thirty years after Ruffian, the nation found itself in another quagmire of lukewarm mediocrity. The thermometer readings measuring healthy productivity and genuine satisfaction were plummeting once again. An ugly war waged in Iraq; every presidential election divided the country; the economy challenged standards-of-living and general dissatisfaction hit another all-time high. Americans were in a "funk" again. It was time for another athletic wonder to distract everyone from the status quo. It was time for the Smarty Jones Show.

When Pat Chapman decided to keep Smarty Jones, after the tragic murder of his first trainer Bob Camac, the choice was driven by a special look in his eye. Call it the "look of eagles" if you will, but there is something about Smarty that sends a message. Some horses know that they are special, some enjoy humankind more than others and some exude confidence. Smarty is keenly aware of his caregivers, can be a trickster of sorts and is not beyond a practical joke on an unsuspecting groom. Many times it's the small gestures such as these that establish bonds between horses and people.

On the track Smarty seemed to understand each aspect of the race, especially the pilgrimage to the winner's circle. On the day of his retirement party, he could not accept the fact that a romp around the track for cheering fans did not end in the winner's circle. As a classic winner, Smarty had his own style and looked for the attention and adulation of the fans. He knew he was good and he wanted everybody else to know it, too. Every time Smarty Jones would cross the finish line, he would pick up his ears — an exclamation point of sorts — a "Look at what I just did!"

When Smarty Jones was making his Triple Crown bid, his name and face were everywhere. The Jockey Club reported more newly-named foals with Smarty in their title. Thousands of children's letters, drawings and the like were delivered to the Chapmans and to Philadelphia Park everyday. The effort was so unusual and unprecedented, that a special book was published to share them with the general population.

In a city that can be seriously-starved for sport's championships, Smarty Jones became the new savior (even with the white star of anointing on his forehead). His arrival from Kentucky was announced by helicopters and police cars. Thousands of his fans lined Street Road to catch a glimpse of their hero — many had come from as far as Chicago, Baltimore, Washington and New York.

On the morning of May 8th more than 8,000 fans lined up at Philadelphia Park for a Smarty Jones workout. Photos, shirts and hats were sold out before the Preakness, and vendors were scrambling on-line to come up with anything Smarty. His charisma and accomplishments had taken the nation by storm. Invitations had come in from President Bush for Smarty to visit the White House, and plans were in the works to change the name of a rather large Philadelphia roadway to Smarty Jones Boulevard.

When Smarty won the Preakness Stakes, it was by the largest margin of victory in the history of that race. Pimlico was filled to capacity and no one went home disappointed. By the time of the Belmont Stakes, national newspapers had recipes for Smarty Parties and special sections with cutout banners and crowns. The total attendance at Belmont that day even exceeded the numbers from the previous year's New York favorite, Funny Cide. There were over 122,000 fans cheering for Smarty. This is an unusual feat in its own right — to have this number of New Yorkers rooting for anything from Philadelphia speaks volumes about Smarty's popularity.

The loss at the Belmont Stakes did little if anything to dim Smarty's high-level popularity. Even retirement has made him even closer to his fan base in a way, as people travel from all over the country to visit him in Kentucky, where daily tours are conducted. Many wonderful stallions stand at Three Chimneys Farm but most fans will tell you that they are there to see "Smarty Jones." During the daily tour, Ann Hayes discusses Smarty with his public. Visitors will gladly tell you that Smarty Jones is the most well-known living Thoroughbred in the world. "Everyone's heard of Smarty Jones!" On any given day, it is perfectly normal for Smarty Jones to receive approximately 40 fan letters, and in a normal month he could receive as many as 1000 letters. His popularity has not dimmed one bit.

In his own home state, Smarty Jones helped to save Pennsylvania racing. Competition from neighboring states' slot machines and gambling casinos had and were taking their toll on Pennsylvania racetracks. As Governor Ed Rendell announced, "Smarty had a lot to do with expanded gaming at racetracks. Smarty reminded people that we were saving a sport in Pennsylvania." Without the slot machines, Pennsylvania may not have had any horseracing industry in ten or fifteen years. By July 28, 2007, the debut of the Smarty Jones Classic, Philadelphia Park was celebrating its first million-dollar day in purses. The positive impact of the slot machines could already be seen.

Few will deny that Smarty worked major miracles for horseracing in his own state and other places, too. In 2004 the commissioner of the National Thoroughbred Racing Association Tim Smith said,

The interesting thing to me is that, even before the Preakness win, for a combination of reasons, the impact was measurably greater–I'd say two or three times–that of Funny Cide, as great as that was last year. The impact is tremendous. Any way you measure it–television ratings, media attention, the horse making the cover of *Sports Illustrated*, and coverage in places you wouldn't traditionally see–it has just been astounding.

The "Smarty Effect" was a wonderful thing for thoroughbred racing at a time when it needed a big boost. Off-tracking betting had taken many people away from the track and horseracing was at a crossroads as some tracks struggled to pay their bills. Following on the heels of Smarty's Pennsylvania presence was Afleet Alex with little Alex Scott's memory and her lemonade stands for childhood cancer. Afleet Alex's dynamic Preakness recovery/win and his Belmont win were thrilling, and brought some new fans onboard. Afleet Alex, too, was sidelined permanently into retirement with an unfortunate injury.

Within months of Smarty's retirement another wonder horse came on the horizon–Barbaro. In 2006 pre-Derby predictions, Barbaro was identified as dynamic. His pedigree abounded in strong performers and there had been success with his sire and dam on both turf and dirt. He was going to be another horse with Pennsylvania roots challenging the strongest three-year-olds at Churchill Downs.

At the 132nd Kentucky Derby, Barbaro's performance was stunning. He blistered the track, left his challengers in the dust and posted the largest margin of victory since Assault of sixty years ago. The media identified Barbaro as another strong Triple Crown contender, and the all too familiar rollercoaster ride of May and June had begun again. More new racing fans were brought on-board because Barbaro was going to be the "real thing." By Preakness Saturday, enthusiasm had reached a fever pitch, and Pimlico was hosting another capacity crowd. No one there was in any way prepared for the horrible twist of fate that was to befall Barbaro. This horse was so large, so strong and so filled with life–why had the racing gods turned their backs once again? It was so similar to Ruffian's fate–capacity crowd, newbie fans, national television and a terrible fracture.

In attending to Barbaro's injury, there were many lessons learned from Ruffian's experience. He would be transported to New Bolton Center, stabilized for overnight and placed into surgery the following day. As the horse van left Pimlico, fans lined the roads and overpasses on the way to Kennett Square, Pennsylvania. At New Bolton Center, fans had driven to the edges of the property to leave flowers, posters, signs, carrots, apples and the like. This trend would continue for the eight months and eight days that Barbaro would continue to fight for his life. Ruffian had only lived for eight hours after her injury–her death came quickly to her adoring fans although it was equally as painful.

For the 132nd Kentucky Derby, the program cover and assorted memorabilia had pictured a large horse streaking to victory. The horse's number was number 8–Barbaro's number in the Derby had been number 8, and he went on to win. In the Preakness, that Barbaro never finished, the winning horse Bernardini wore number 8. And later in the Belmont Stakes, the winning horse Jazil also wore number 8. On the 29th of January, the day of Barbaro's death, the Pennsylvania winning lottery number was 8-8-8. It certainly is a big coincidence, but an interesting one.

Many new fans were attracted to Barbaro and to "horse issues" after Barbaro's injury. The media coverage of his injury and recuperation was so thorough that fans wanted daily updates. Many connected with timwoolleyracing.com several times a day to hear the latest news via Michael Matz, Barbaro's trainer, who visited early every morning, and then passed updates on to webmaster Alex Brown. Others used the website of the University of Pennsylvania's School of Veterinary Medicine just to keep informed.

The Jacksons and the New Bolton Staff were overwhelmed with cards, letters and calls. Kennett Square Florist brought trays of goodies for nurses, doctors and staff, as well as more flowers and baskets than any one person could enjoy in a lifetime. These were daily happenings for months and months. The posters on the outside fence grew and gifts were left on a daily basis. Visitors from all over the country drove to New Bolton Center just to see where Barbaro was being treated. There were physical ups-and-downs for Barbaro over those months and each news conference became a national happening.

There were individuals who felt that Barbaro had touched their lives in many ways. Some people with very serious illnesses wrote to share their thoughts about Barbaro inspiring them, others asked to see him before they would pass. Many people sent religious articles: prayer cards, statues, rosaries, medals and pictures. The ruler of Dubai U.A.E., Sheikh Mohammed himself sent urns of water from the River Jordan–acknowledged by many as a symbol of health and vitality. A local university professor who had a piece of the bone of St. Francis of Assisi came to New Bolton to place the relic on Barbaro. Many websites offered fans the opportunity to write a greeting to Barbaro. Churchill Downs, Belmont Park, Pimlico and other racetracks prepared huge four foot by eight foot Get Well cards for fans to sign. These were in turn shipped to New Bolton Center and displayed in their front lobby. There seemed to be no end to America reaching out to Barbaro.

Since Barbaro's death there has been a movement which is called the "Barbaro Effect." Many horse-related issues that came to the forefront during his hospitalization are now being examined and, hopefully, resolved in a positive way. Barbaro and Ruffian did not get the miracles which everyone so desperately wanted. As Gretchen Jackson said, "You are not supposed to fall in love with a horse" Well, America did. America fell in love with these three horses especially...and others, too. The real miracle may be that they touched our lives so deeply, and now we are better because of them.

Equine Injuries: Soundness v. Brilliance

In the wake of Barbaro's breakdown at the 2006 Preakness Stakes, there has been a media blitz on race track injuries. Many of the fractures and maladies of the great horse stars from the past have been discussed, and the public has demonstrated much more of an interest in this side of the industry. To learn that the great Secretariat lost his life to laminitis, hit a sensitive nerve with Barbaro's public as they watched his eight month battle to live. Through the spring of 2007, there have been any number of recent stars that are being retired. Some have serious injuries and others do not. It seems to be the tenor of the times for many successful thoroughbreds to have short-lived careers.

Back in the time of Ruffian, it was the modern Golden Age of Racing. She was part of a long list of very successful thoroughbreds which were attracting more and more of the public to the race track. The timing of her injury was terrible in the sense that many of her followers were newly-interested fans, who found her charisma and appeal to be magnetic. Some of these new converts never returned to the track after her death. For others it was an ugly, up-close-and-personal encounter with the risks associated with thoroughbred racing.

On the evening of July 6th, 1975, most of New York went to bed with the belief that the filly would be saved and awoke to the grim details of her surgery and death. In the ensuing weeks, months and years, there has been a rash of articles addressing every angle of her breakdown and ultimate death. Could she have been saved? Why did this tragedy happen? Could anything be done to prevent it? Answers to these questions could fill as many books as there are opinions in this regard. What has aided our understanding many years later are statements from the persons who were *really* there–the doctors who cared for her on a daily basis and on the evening of her surgery.

As Ruffian broke from the gate she struck her ankle on the starting gate which probably caused a hairline fracture. When this author spoke with Mr. Frank Y. Whiteley, he confirmed that this had been the case and it was greatly exacerbated by her pounding on this ankle for the next 100 yards.

The first veterinarian to reach Ruffian on the track was Dr. Manuel Gilman who was the chief examining veterinarian of the New York Racing Association. Dr. Gilman had seen and measured Ruffian as a two-year old. His comments were,

Perhaps it is unfair to compare a two-year-old filly with a thoroughbred sometimes called 'the horse of the century,' but physically Ruffian gets the measurement calls over Secretariat....And I'd say Ruffian is the closest thing to being the perfect filly I've ever seen. As a matter of fact, I've never heard anyone who could fault her in any manner.

Dr. Gilman had measured Secretariat with a tape measure at the same stage of his two-year-old year. He went on to explain,

These measurements are not intended in any manner to reflect the respective racing abilities of Ruffian and Secretariat. Such things come under a different heading. Secretariat is another magnificent creature physically, but does not come up to Ruffian's standards. I could employ all sorts of superlatives but words can't really describe her.

During her time at Belmont Park, Dr. Gilman had come to know Ruffian very well. He described her as very, very healthy. Even in the pre-racing physical before the Great Match Race, Gilman found her to be totally healthy in every way. She was a dominant filly weighing almost 1200 pounds as compared with her opponent, Foolish Pleasure, who weighed 1020 pounds. She stood almost 16 hands 3, where Foolish Pleasure stood 15 hands 3. By racing standards and filly standards she was a big girl, who had never been headed or beaten in any race.

The regular veterinarian for Ruffian had been Dr. James Prendergast. He had tended to her splints in her two-year-old year and the hairline fracture which sent her into stall rest after the Spinaway in August 1974. As a three-year old she came back with a flourish and Dr. Prendergast was an overseer of her general health and soundness.

Both veterinarians were present the evening of Ruffian's injury. Dr. Gilman was the first to reach her on the track and Dr. Prendergast quickly followed to the scene in his car. It had taken Jacinto Vasquez almost 50 yards to get the filly to stop. During that stretch she had ground her broken skin and bone into the dirt, grit and gravel. Dr. Gilman applied an air cast, which ruptured in minutes due to the tremendous force behind the hemorrhaging leg. This was replaced as they transported her back to her stall. Dr. Prendergast and Dr. Alex Harthill, Whiteley's friend from Kentucky and Ruffian's veterinarian in South Carolina, remained in the stall as radiographs were being taken. Dr. Prendergast administered the needed drugs for coagulation and infection. Anti-histamines, tranquilizers and narcotic medications were also given by Dr. Prendergast before he moved to his car for additional supplies. While Dr. Prendergast was out of the stall, Dr. William Reed, who had never treated the filly moved to her right side, and gave her an injection. To this day no one was ever told what it was but it greatly excited the filly.

At this point, the decision was made to move her to Dr. Reed's Equine Hospital across the street. She was clearly in tremendous pain and moving in and out of shock. As readily as possible, Ruffian was placed under anesthesia and the challenge began. Both proximal sesamoids of the right front ankle had been pulverized and the leg was contaminated from the dirt and gravel. The surgeons worked vigorously to rearrange the bone fragments and insert drains wherever possible. At the conclusion of the surgery Ruffian had been fitted with a forty-pound cast and placed into recovery. From that point on the rest is history, ending with her being euthanized at 2:20 am, July 7, 1975.

The week after Ruffian's tragic death Dr. Alex Harthill wrote an article for *The Daily Racing Form.* In the lengthy analysis Dr. Harthill identified some salient points. The filly had been revived from the dead twice during the operation, the original fracture was one one-hundredth as serious as the final result from her continued running, her violent reaction to waking up from the anesthesia caused more hemorrhaging and fractures and the surgeons were left with no options at 2:00 in the morning. When all was said and done, Ruffian was euthanized.

For Dr. Gilman the original diagnosis of Ruffian's injury, when he treated her on the track, was accurate. She had pulverized both sesamoids, and then greatly aggravated the leg by her constant running. There was nothing controversial in Dr. Gilman's assessment of the filly's injuries,

She had been going so fast and was so full of herself–she was in the race of her life–that she kept running on the fracture, grinding, grinding, grinding the bones. It was an unbelievable injury. The ligaments were shattered. The bones were like pieces of glass.

Dr. Gilman participated in the surgery with the others. As Ruffian's condition worsened he was aware of her temperament which many believed only exacerbated her difficult prognosis. His comment was, "There is no other explanation. [It was] Just one bad step."

This author spoke with both Mike Bell, Ruffian's assistant trainer, and Dr. James Prendergast, her regular veterinarian. Both concurred that her temperament would be a terrible obstacle for any type of medical intervention. She had not tolerated a cast at age two and was totally "independent and free-spirited." Dr. Prendergast did believe that the improvements in veterinary medicine have been significant. "We didn't have the antibiotics, the analgesics, or the knowledge that is currently available. She would have suffered a fate worse than her tragic death. It would have been just prolonged, painful and inhumane." The main reason why Ruffian was brought to surgery was because of who she was. Any other animal would have been euthanized on the track.

By the middle of July 1975, there were conspiracy theories out there. In the fifties we had James Dean, in the sixties the assassination of JFK, and in the seventies Ruffian's breakdown. Some believed that the track had been altered to make it faster and hence more dangerous. Others cited the appearance of groupings of birds on the track which flew up in Ruffian's face to frighten her. Both of these were dismissed by factual information from eyewitnesses and track officials.

What has remained all of these years is the tragedy of her loss. She was a one-in-a-million horse that had legend and greatness written all over her. What she accomplished was spectacular, but the question will always remain, "If she had never been injured, what would have been?"

There was greatness in her pedigree. In an interview with Anne Peters, at Three Chimneys Farm, this author discussed Ruffian's pedigree and breakdown at great length. My questions addressed any unsoundness in her bloodlines which could have suggested or predicted her tragic injury. What must be kept in mind is the weight of these animals, the fragility of their legs and the speeds at which they run.

"How sound was Ruffian? was posed as a question to Anne Peters. Anne replied,

She was a breakdown waiting to happen...I describe her as crystal, perfect but fragile. It came from both sides of her family. Her entire pedigree was rife with unsoundness, but incredible brilliance. When you have unsoundness and brilliance at the same time, you have got to give it a chance.

Both of Ruffian's grand sires, Bold Ruler and Native Dancer, had some issues with injuries and fractures. Anne Peters went on to discuss Ruffian's ancestors.

Reviewer [Ruffian's sire]–was a brilliant racehorse who was always working his way to the top of his class, and then he would break down. He did that three years, climb to the top of the division then go wrong in the same leg each time. That was typical with the Bold Rulers. They were known to be very brittle but game as could be. They were very heavy-topped horses–a lot of muscle. They were gladiators on toothpick legs—some of them could handle it and some of them couldn't. Secretariat [Ruffian's uncle] was so heavily muscled, even more than Bold Ruler, but he was sound although some of his offspring were not. Their legs couldn't handle the weight....Even

Secretariat was a gamble–those Bold Rulers don't hold together. He defied the odds.

On Ruffian's dam side was Shenanigans by Native Dancer. Anne continued,

Native Dancer on her other side had ankle problems. Shenanigans [her mother] had knee problems. Native Dancer was a very large horse and you could expect ankle problems as he pounded down on those ankles....Almost every part of Ruffian was set up for potential trouble. Whiteley held her together the best he could. If given a choice to run in that Match Race, I think he would have said, "No."...In this sport, brilliance and soundness are a trade-off. It is very rare to find a very sound horse that is as fast and as talented as some of these champions. There is a delicate balancing point.

There was no real predicting Ruffian's injury per se because she had done very well in her ten previous races. In footage of the Match Race, one can see her strike her right ankle very hard against the starting gate. That could happen on any given day at any given time. The force and intensity of the next 45 seconds were her undoing. If it happened in a workout or in a paddock, the result may have been different.

As far as saving her today, this author discussed that with Dr. Dean Richardson at New Bolton Center. Dr. Richardson explained some key points to consider,

If Ruffian's fracture happened today, the chances of her surviving would be far better, far better than they were thirty years ago....but despite all that, with all the advances that have been made, no one with a lick of common sense could say that Ruffian definitely would have been saved. One, I wasn't there to see how severe the injury was, and two, even if it were something that I thought had a good chance, a fair number of those don't succeed. We should be able to save about 75% of the horses when both sesamoids have been fractured. But if you happen to be a part of the 25% that doesn't make it, that's still a failure.

In addition to her terrible injury, Ruffian was one of those horses, which would have benefited from a recovery pool. This was used many times with Barbaro as he recovered from anesthesia. Ruffian further injured herself as she awakened in her "fight and flight response." Interestingly enough, both of her parents were dead within two years of her death. Both had undergone relatively common surgical procedures yet died from the effects of poor recovery from anesthesia.

In the final analysis, Ruffian gave her all, and it cost her everything—her very lifeblood. As Bill Lyon, of *The Philadelphia Inquirer* so aptly said, "Ruffian became a victim of her own gallantry….And that's what made her such a great filly…her determination….a glossy, gallant filly taught us all a little something about dignity."

In the case of Smarty Jones, he had overcome untold hurdles before even getting into his first race. A freak accident with the starting gate in July 2003, almost cost him his life and at the very least his left eye. The horse lay unconscious with blood pouring from his nose and mouth. He became an emergency case for Dr. Patricia Hogan at the New Jersey Equine Center who was a medical genius with his skull fractures and soft tissue injuries. Dubbed Quasimodo by the staff because of his grotesque appearance, Smarty's strong will and gutsy determination brought him through the ordeal seemingly unscathed. After several months of rest and rehabilitation, he was able to enter a gate again and trounce the field by 7-1/2 lengths in his maiden race at Philadelphia Park on November 9th, just four months later.

During Smarty's first six races, he proved that he could beat the speed and outstay the stayers. He went to the Derby as the sixth undefeated candidate in 130 years and the first since Seattle Slew in 1977. As Smarty's talent emerged he captivated the entire racing world, but this did not happen overnight. Many of the sportwriters criticized his size, his pedigree, his Philadelphia roots, his previous racing venues and even his name [Sorry, Mrs. Chapman, I know that it was your mother's nickname].

As a two year old, Smarty had missed months of racing due to his accident in July. When the other precocious two-year-olds were getting their names in lights and on pre-Derby betting sheets, Smarty was trying to find his way around Arkansas. His campaign from November 9th, 2003 to April 10th, 2004 was a very intense one for a horse having had a very serious accident in July.

With the beginning of the Triple Crown races, the pace greatly intensified. The short periods between the races and the media circus that accompanies the total experience are draining on everyone involved, even the horses. Smarty was shipped to Keeneland, Churchill Downs, Pimlico and finally Belmont in about a six-week period. This is arduous at best for anyone and has had some people suggest that the Triple Crown challenge has almost become unfair to all involved, there are many trainers who will do the Derby, skip the Preakness and move on to the Belmont.

What we must remember about the intensity which has come to accompany the Triple Crown races–this title is a recent invention. There was no Triple Crown of races until 1950. Even though Charles Hatton created the expression in the thirties, there was no such award. All of the early winners, Sir Barton, Gallant Fox, Count Fleet, Omaha, War Admiral, Whirlaway, Assault, and Citation were grandfathered this award. Each year from December 1950 on, a different "older winner" was awarded the beautiful trophy until the Thoroughbred Racing Association caught up with the eight that had previously won those three designated races. Had the crown existed eighty years ago, even Samuel Riddle may have entered Man O' War in the Kentucky Derby. The only horses that competed for this titled trophy, as an existing award, were those after 1950.

We had to wait 25 years for the first winner after Citation. The triumvirate in the seventies included: Secretariat, Seattle Slew and Affirmed. Even thirty years ago when they competed, it did not have the intense media blitz that the last ten years have created. Now, here we are in 2008 with a thirty-year drought. The question needs to be addressed, "Is it too difficult?" In 2004, it may not have appeared to have been too exhausting for Smarty but he did pay a dear price after the campaign was over. He was the only horse that ran in all three Triple Crown races that year.

After the Belmont Stakes, Smarty was entitled to a very well-deserved rest. Plans were being made for his next race, and some of the choices included: the Haskell, the Travers, the Pennsylvania Derby and the Breeders' Cup in the fall. Many of the horses that Smarty had beaten were ready for a rematch or two and the fans were reeling with Smarty mania.

When Smarty returned to Philadelphia Park from Elmont, New York, serious soreness was noted on all four of his feet. It is not particularly uncommon for this to happen but the reasons for and the duration of the injury can be far more complex. He was treated with stall rest, and many horses recover in that time from general soreness or surface bruising. If a horse responds to that timely rest, trainers will generally reintroduce them to modified activity little-by-little.

When this soreness or bruising was announced as a Smarty Jones's injury, one veterinarian commented that this was a minor injury and that the horse would be back in thirty days. That was the only statement which some of the media heard, and Smarty's condition was quoted as "recovering from a minor injury." When weeks passed and he did not respond to rest and treatment, things had become far more serious but those same media friends wouldn't hear any of it. The belief was that Smarty and the Chapmans were in a sense looking for an excuse to retire the horse, which was the farthest thing from the truth. In the contract with Three Chimneys, Smarty was scheduled to race in his fourth year if John Servis and his veterinarians deemed that he was healthy enough to do that. Even when he arrived at Three Chimneys, timely reevaluations were done to see if Smarty were improving and ready to turn a positive corner in his ankle problems.

As Smarty's condition did not improve, three different veterinarians' opinions were sought independently. After a scintigraphic evaluation at Mid-Atlantic Equine Center, Smarty's prognosis was micro cracks of the distal palmar at the base of the cannon bone which were severe and damaging the cartilage at the base of that part of the bone. The scintigraphic evaluation indicated bone activity that was both continual and intense. The healing process was unable to keep up with the damage. The racing that Smarty had done so intensely over the previous four or five months contributed to the overwhelming bone stress. Smarty's legs had lost the cushioning effect leaving him with minimal ability to absorb the shock and stress that breezing created. At the time of his arrival at Mid-Atlantic Equine Center, Dr. Peter Brousum told this author that Smarty was barely able to jog.

This author spoke with Dr. Dean Richardson, at New Bolton Center. Dr. Richardson greatly elaborated on this type of injury.

A Thoroughbred horse's fetlock is the most vulnerable organ essentially in the horse's entire body. The fetlock in a Thoroughbred race horse is the weak link in a horse of that occupation. The fact that he was diagnosed with bone bruising is, the important thing to understand, is just one part of a number of things that are going on in the fetlock at the same time. So, if he were really bruising the bone on what's called the distal condylar, the lower back part of the cannon bone, which is again very common,....you have to pretty much accept that if he's doing that, and if it's severe, he is also damaging the cartilage, which is the lining on the outside of the bone....I think anybody, who has been around horses, knows that when it gets sore with the fetlock with damage like that, some of them will progress on to develop more arthritis....If you go on with a horse like that, they can end up suffering a much more serious injury....Some of those horses will be back in thirty days; other ones, it's just the first step in a sequence of events that's going to result in their ankle deteriorating.....It can be a career-ending injury for a high level horse. That's another thing that people have to recognize. If you're talking about a multiple grade I stakes winner, that's going to be a stallion, you don't push a horse like that beyond a certain point. They have nothing left to prove, and there is too much risk involved in pushing them ahead farther. There is no reason to do it.

After seeking many opinions, including the original veterinarian who had spoken with the media initially before examining the horse, the Chapmans were forced to withdraw Smarty from his projected racing schedule and announce his retirement on the 2nd of August, 2004. The entire fan base was greatly disappointed and many of the media were very angry. The story was portrayed by some journalists as a "grab the money and run," scenario, which caused the Chapmans a great deal of criticism and a large measure of personal pain. In the succeeding years, there have been a number of Triple Crown race stars which have been retired with minimal, if any, media backlash. That was not the case with Smarty Jones and the Chapman family.

In reviewing Smarty Jones there are some very interesting things to note. Much of the publicity that surrounded Smarty's emergence after the Arkansas Derby referred to "a little blue collar horse from the wrong side of the tracks." Nothing is farther from the truth. Smarty's sire is Elusive Quality who is very high-prized stallion. He is the son of Gone West (another high class stakes winner and coveted sire) and his grand sire is the famed Mr. Prospector. Both sides of the pedigree go back to Triple Crown winners and even Ruffian's ancestors are in his pedigree. He has Bold Ruler and Native Dancer, her grand sires, even Foolish Pleasure shows up on his dam's side. Both Smarty's dam and grand dam were stakes winners and there are not too many horses that have that in their pedigree.

This author asked Anne Peters, of Three Chimneys Farm, about Smarty's speed and stamina. Her comments were:

Smarty hit a cruising speed so high and so efficiently, and that is the key to stamina–to hit that cruising speed and keep going without laboring. At Belmont that day (Belmont Stakes) he basically ran five different races. It was a psychological war, not a staying war.

The next generation of little Smarties will begin racing in 2008. Anne commented on their potential,

From Smarty's babies…he is such a powerhouse, and he is perfectly balanced. I'm expecting great two-year olds. He has great muscling and his babies have the size. He's getting big babies. When they were coming out, they were big–Elusive Quality [his sire] was big. As I see it, the perception that he was "too small," came when that nearly seven foot man [Bill Foster–barn manager] used to hot walk him at Philadelphia Park. Smarty has grown to 16 hands, which is average. He is the same size as Storm Cat, A.P.Indy and Gone West. He's actually bigger than Distorted Humor, and no one shunned him as a sire because he's small. Smarty's babies, however, are big and well built.

In his position as stallion at Three Chimneys Farm, Smarty gets his daily exercise in the paddock although no one has been able to ride him since June of 2004 due to his leg problems. He has had ultrasounds and other nuclear tests done periodically, since he has been in Kentucky, to assess the extent of the deteriorating cartilage in his feet. Through all of this, Smarty is a happy horse and a wonderful goodwill ambassador for all who come to see him for visits or tours.

From the moment of Barbaro's tragic injury on May 20, 2006 to the day of his death on January 29, 2007, the American public experienced a mini-course on equine fractures. Dr. Dean Richardson masterfully guided the media corps and the fan base through all of these intricacies in "layman's language" and with infinite patience. A very complicated and challenging surgery was completed the day after the Preakness Stakes, and a "Barbaro Watch" began that lasted for 8 months and 8 days. During all of this time the public was kept well informed. We viewed X-rays, watched pool recoveries, observed the support sling, compared casts, researched laminitis and accompanied Barbaro on his outside walks. The doors of the New Bolton Center of the University of Pennsylvania School of Veterinary Medicine were opened for the world to see its inner workings, and this exposure was probably more successful than any highly touted and pricey public relations campaign.

As Barbaro made his misstep, the more knowledgeable horse observers among us knew that it was a very serious injury. As Dr. Dean Richardson watched the horror unfolding he knew that it was going to be bad, but he also knew that if the colt were to have surgery, it would not be that day. If nothing else came from Ruffian's ordeal, it was the realization that the horse's systems needed to settle before anesthesia and surgery could be attempted. As Barbaro was transported to Kennett Square, Pennsylvania, plans were in the works to hospitalize and stabilize him as readily as possible. All of this was accomplished perfectly and he had a very restful and relatively pain-free evening.

In discussions of Barbaro's fracture, Dr. Richardson compared it to a bag of crushed ice. He sought to stabilize the area of the fracture by using a single LCP (locking compression plate) and a series of titanium screws (27 all together). The leg would be casted and X-rayed periodically to check the positioning and integrity of the implants. Over the ensuing weeks, efforts would be made to keep Barbaro as pain-free as possible and to encourage him to use all of his legs for even weight distribution.

Numerous press conferences were held early on to apprise the general public of the horse's physical well-being and his amazingly positive response to the entire experience. Through the months of May, June and early July, casts were changed, reports were positive and Barbaro responded well. By the middle of July the dreaded diagnosis of laminitis was reported in a specially-scheduled newscast. The news threw Barbaro's public into a panic. The horse had come through a terribly-compromising surgery and recovery only to be smitten by this silent killer. As the nation learned more about the insidiousness of the disease, everyone feared for Barbaro's continued survival. The disease with its terrible pain and problems had taken the great Secretariat. There were no assurances and chances were looking dimmer by the minute.

To everyone's surprise, Barbaro rallied past that July episode and things seemed to swing on an upward trend for a time. The horse was eating very well, showed strong vital signs and finally stood, without a cast, on that once-shattered leg. Many were beginning to think that the battle may have been won but the haunting reminders of Dr. Richardson were always lurking in the background. Dr. Richardson still characterized Barbaro's survival as a "coin toss," and only months and months of growth in the left hind hoof would erase those doubts.

Through the fall of 2006 and into December, there were casts placed on Barbaro's hind limbs for greater support. The laminitic foot was fraught with issues, and the good leg (the Preakness fracture) was experiencing extra strain coming off of the painful left hind foot. Barbaro was responding reasonably well to these casts and procedures, displayed a good appetite, had not contracted any additional infections and was going outside for grazing as the weather permitted. Dr. Richardson described him many times as a very "happy horse," that was taking all of these issues in stride, a large one at that.

In early December, suggestions were made that Barbaro might be moved to a more forgiving climate than the harsh Pennsylvania winters, if he were stable enough to do that. This announcement sent many positive vibes across the airwaves as the Barbaro faithful relaxed just a bit, hoping that the horse may be turning a real corner, and moving in a totally positive direction. Over the weeks before Christmas this did not really amount to anything, but the laminitis was still active and the hoof was neither growing well nor correctly. We were still a long way away from the answer that everyone so desperately wanted.

After the first of the year the laminitic foot was getting sorer and placing additional demands on the "good leg." Barbaro's appetite was very good, vital signs were positive and his disposition seemed fine. As the month progressed there were more issues with the left foot. The media may not have reported these developments to the same degree as they had in the summer and fall, because it wasn't a case of something negative happening. It was more a case of what wasn't happening. Barbaro's issues weren't going away. During those last ailing 48 hours the problem had hit a real high point—he had run out of miracles and the house of cards was unraveling. For the first time, the horse was in real pain and it was affecting his weight distribution and his disposition. By the 29th of January he was not himself, and all of his legs were beset in one way or another. The front feet, for the first time, were showing signs of laminitis and the horse had not been able to get up or down by his own volition for two days. Pins had been inserted into the right hind leg for additional support, when an abscess was detected. There were no good legs left, and it was time to address what quality of life existed for Barbaro–very little if any. It was time.

This author is an avid F.O.B. (Fan of Barbaro), and had harbored concerns about the apparent sudden decline of Barbaro at the end of his life. In an interview with Dr. Dean Richardson, these concerns were shared, and Dr. Richardson reiterated some facts, which helped in gaining a larger and clearer picture of Barbaro's final days.

The horse's left hind foot was always a problem. If you go back, it was a problem over and over again. He wasn't going to survive with his left foot the way it was. It wasn't growing properly; we had to try and get his left hind foot to grow properly. It is categorically incorrect to conclude the reason he didn't make it, was because of the cast on his hind foot. It was a problem. It wasn't getting any better, and he was getting by. By December and early January, he was already getting sorer in his left hind foot. It wasn't growing properly.

When asked why it was necessary to cast Barbaro's right hind foot again, Dr. Richardson replied, "The cast put back on the right hind was to protect that limb because it was becoming overloaded due to the increasing lameness on his left hind."

During his illness and ultimate death, Barbaro showed so much to so many people. He was a valiant warrior whose stall became somewhat of a pulpit and many people all over the country and the world gleaned wisdom from his courage, determination and strength. He will be remembered for the example that he provided for all of us.

When this author spoke with Anne Peters at Three Chimneys Farm, where Dynaformer (Barbaro's sire) stands, we discussed Barbaro's breakdown. Many had felt that he was injured because of a collision with Brother Derek. Others had dismissed this notion after film review. Anne's comments were, "What happened to Barbaro? Probably a bad step. He was really "on" before the race. I saw him so finely tuned that day. He was ready to go...delighted with life." Barbaro's grand sire Hail to Reason had fractured his sesamoids on a Sunday morning workout, but had not moved after the injury. He was casted and survived. No two horses may respond the same way to being injured and so much hangs in the balance as far as their treatment options, based on their response to injury. With Ruffian her reaction was her virtual undoing. Barbaro, on the other hand, showed remarkable patience and self-control as he waited on the track for assistance.

As a further reinforcement of Barbaro's health and soundness, this author was fortunate to speak with Dr. Kathy Anderson, Barbaro's regular veterinarian. She commented on how healthy the horse had been prior to his misstep on Preakness Saturday. It had not ever been necessary to X-ray him for any reason prior to that day.. He was a strong, vibrant and healthy animal, that had never been ill or injured.

In his pedigree Barbaro showed great strength and stamina. Both sides are strong, with such notable sires and grand sires as Carson City, Mr. Prospector, Roberto and Hail to Reason. Among his distant ancestors are more greats, Nasrullah, Bull Lea (Citation's sire) and Native Dancer, just to name a few. The bloodlines were strong and the limited picture of his greatness, that we saw, suggested that he could run all day, if only time and circumstances had not robbed us of that distant vision of greatness.

No one will disagree with the fact that thoroughbred racing has changed dramatically from what it was fifty or sixty years ago. Back in 1918 the great Exterminator started 100 times in his career and won half of those starts. In 1948, Citation raced 20 times and won 19 out of the 20 starts plus the Triple Crown races. These are statistics which cannot even be suggested to any of the Triple Crown trainers or owners from the last ten years. The great Seabiscuit had 89 starts to his credit. Back in the '40's the average number of career starts was between 50 and 60. Moving into the '60's the number had shifted to 26.2, and by the '80's it was down to 21.2. At the conclusion of the Smarty Jones campaign, the average number had dipped to 6.2 career starts. Many of these horses are not around long enough for folks to learn their names or follow their schedules.

There are many theories on limited career starts which address these declines. Some horses run too early as two-year-olds. Are there too many races on hardened dirt? Has year-round racing jeopardized the industry? Are too many medications masking a larger problem? Surely money drives many retirement-to-stud decisions, but not all. One other factor, which may be affecting the over-all fragility of the equine athlete, is the cessation of large quantities of limestone in the Kentucky water sources. Back in the '60's, city sewers and water lines were extended to rural Lexington farms. Prior to that time, the horses drank the lime-stone-enriched spring water. What kind of a difference has this made? We may never know but it is something to think about long term.

Medical Advancements

It has been thirty-three years since the death of Ruffian. Many things have changed with respect to veterinary protocols and surgery techniques. There have been articles addressing the ability to save her from her horrific injury with new information and through sophisticated technology. From one perspective, Douglas Herthel, founder of the Alamo Pintado Equine Research Clinic in Los Olives, California, believed in 1995 that the new technologies and state-of-the-art equipment could have made a difference.

Dr. Herthel has suggested that if Ruffian's injury happened twenty years later, here are some of the changes that probably would have been made. Doctors would have used a *Kimsey splint* (one of these was used on Barbaro) to replace the air cast that was applied to Ruffian. These splints thoroughly immobilize the entire injured leg and are able to preserve the health of the arteries. With the arteries compromised, the horse could experience postoperative circulation problems.

During the surgery, veterinarians now monitor blood-gases through surgery. As Herthel related, "Horses are monitored with *blood-gas analysis*…You are able to maintain the optimum physiological conditions in their blood as far as oxygen and carbon dioxide." This balance aids in keeping better circulation within the muscles. As the horse awakes from anesthesia, there is better muscle coordination and fewer instances of panic.

A third innovation would be the use of a *pulse oxymeter*. This device is placed on the tongue of the anesthetized horse during the entire surgery. It will provide continuous measurement of the levels of arterial oxygen saturation in the blood as well as the pulse rate.

As an effective means of repairing joints, the *interlocking-nail procedure* is used. The veterinary surgeon will insert a titanium rod the length of the cannon bone and into the pasterns. By doing this the ankle structures are effectively locked together.

Another intervention that assists with the surgery is *atricurium*. Delivering drugs for muscle relaxation is known to be a very delicate process. This acts as a muscle-contraction blocking agent which allows for a safe and relaxed paralysis. This aids in keeping the anesthetized horse still and calm until the anesthesia has worn off.

Unlike Barbaro, Ruffian had a great deal of difficulty with the anesthesia process. Dr. Dean Richardson in an interview with this author presented many insights into Ruffian's difficulties.

Anesthesia for horses thirty years ago was vastly inferior to what's done today. The anesthetic is different, the pre-medication protocols are different, and the monitoring is immensely different....It is far safer than it was thirty years ago and...it would be extraordinarily rare nowadays, almost unheard of, for a horse to have the type of recovery which she had. It just doesn't happen.

What exists for the horses of today are three unique methods of recovery after surgery. As the nation watched the blindfolded Barbaro being hoisted in a large sling from a rubber raft floating in a 30,000 gallon pool, they were introduced to the pool recovery system at New Bolton Center in Kennett Square, Pennsylvania. This variation is one-of-a-kind in the entire world. As Dr. Richardson explained,

It's very straight forward. The pool recovery system is designed to help prevent horses from injuring themselves when they go from being in recumbency to standing up. When they are waking up, they do not have control of their neuro-muscular faculties, the brain isn't working right, their muscles aren't working right, and yet they are frantic to get to their feet and run away....The point of it is the anesthesia, you put a blindfold on them, you lift them up and put them down, and they are able to stand up. They never have to go from being down to being up.

This pool recovery system is employed for more sophisticated surgeries in which there is a greater risk for the animal. On an annual basis, it would not be unusual for this system to be used between sixty and seventy times; the most common instance would be Thoroughbreds with medial condylar fractures, where there is a much higher risk for post-surgery injury.

A second option available for post-surgical recovery is the Anderson sling, named for its inventor Charles Anderson. As Denise Steffanus from *The Thoroughbred Times* explained, the sling utilizes "a specially designed apparatus attached to a hydraulic frame and power supply that lifts and stabilizes a horse after surgery." The sling permits the horse's weight to be distributed evenly by supporting its skeletal system without compromising its chest and abdomen.

One of Anderson's collaborators during the design was Dr. John Madigan from the UC-Davis School of Veterinary Medicine. Dr. Madigan said, "A significant factor in whether a horse lives or dies after surgery is whether he can get up. If a horse has to lie down for two or three weeks, complications arise." By design, the Anderson sling may be utilized for weeks and months in the case of animals that are unable to bear weight for a lengthy period. In the case of Barbaro's struggle with laminitis, there were a number of times that the sling was used to minimize his weight-bearing. Some horses adjust better than others. Some horses are able to sleep well within the sling and this is a significant factor in terms of a full recovery.

A final alternative for post-surgical recoveries is the padded recovery suite which may be seen at Texas A&M University large animal hospital. A catwalk is placed above a grouping of four padded recovery stalls, which permits an anesthesiologist to observe four different animals waking from anesthesia. Within each stall is a large hoist that would raise the animal in a sling if necessary, and there are cuts within the walls that serve as shelter to protect attendants from fractious animals. The stalls are thickly padded with as many as eight inches of covered foam padding. Animals are carefully observed and interventions may be employed as needed.

Since Ruffian's tragic accident many new innovations and inventions have become part of state-of-the-art veterinary hospitals. Efforts have been made to reduce the risks whenever possible, and so many more surgeries have positive resolutions. Animals are stabilized before surgery to a much greater degree, (for

Barbaro a twenty-four hour wait) and many other basic aspects of the horse's care are tremendously improved. As Dr. Dean Richardson, from New Bolton Center, reported, "The implants are better, the surgical techniques are far better, the recovery systems and antibiotics are better. Every single aspect of the surgery is vastly superior to what it was thirty years ago."

Legacy

In the early stages of the book, this author defined a hero as "an epitome of strength and valor, who accomplishes incredible feats in noble and compelling ways... he/she elevates legions of followers to new and greater heights by virtue of his/her charisma." After all that has been said few would question the hero status of Ruffian, Smarty Jones and Barbaro. We are very fortunate that Smarty is still with us, but in no way should his contribution be lessened. These horses have made large PR statements to the sport of thoroughbred racing, and have become "consciences" for the sport going forward. If the sport will continue to exist, hope to flourish and look to a rejuvenation, there are some pieces of unfinished business that must be addressed.

In the Hemingway tradition, the hero is expected to meet his or her earthly end. This is part of the "hero thing," and for the guts and glory a price must be paid. In the losses of Ruffian and Barbaro, the public was drawn in as never before. Even people who did not understand the sport, took the time for more than a casual interest. The survival of thoroughbred racing going forward is going to be driven by attention to the issues that their deaths brought to the forefront.

For Ruffian, her legacy surrounds the medical advances that were not there for her–but will help to save the lives of others. Barbaro benefited from some of the mistakes that were made in her case. As he grazed in the warm October sunshine on a healed right hind leg, that was part of her legacy. Other contributions to the industry were medications for horses—some very beneficial, some very abused, but the concept did not come to the fore until after her death. A third and valuable contribution is the modern facilities that now exist with pools for recovery, rather than padded stalls. All of these things have made a real difference for others.

The legacy of Barbaro is clearly a better life for horses now. The issues of anti-slaughter, rescue, track surfaces, track injuries, general accountability and responsibility must be dealt with in timely and effective ways. Greater money has been devoted to medical research for a variety of diseases, with laminitis leading the list. Many of the tracks across the country have established funds or scholarships in his name and donations continue to pour in to University of Pennsylvania School of Veterinary Medicine. He didn't die in vain. It's all about getting the message out to the public who can make a difference. As Alex Brown, of then timwoolleyracing.com and now alexbrownracing.com, so aptly said, "Barbaro has really given us a good kick in the withers. Horse racing can't just do things the same old way. People care now. People are looking." Since September 2006, his group (Fans of Barbaro) has rescued over 1900 horses, and raised more than $800,000 in donations.

The legacies of Barbaro and Ruffian are not about sentimentality. On the other hand, they are driving change. As Staci Hancock, a longtime activist against slaughter houses, has said, "I think what Barbaro has done is show that the American people really do care about horses." Not only do they care about horses, but they are willing to undertake many things to improve their lots in life. Many of the suggested changes have been begun, like track surfaces, but others will require more of a gargantuan effort for a long period of time. It's about changing the culture, and that doesn't happen overnight.

Another reason that the public has embraced these heroes is because of their innocence and sincerity. Many of today's sports stars are poor role models with over-inflated egos and tarnished integrity. Horses on the other hand are basically simple creatures that are honest, hard-working and loyal. They ask for so little and look to us for their care—much like children. What they give in return far outweighs our efforts.

For Barbaro, the torch is being passed to his two full brothers: Nicanor, a yearling, and little LaVille (yet unnamed) who was born in April 2007. As of this writing LaVille was bred once again to Dynaformer in May and another foal should arrive to add to the family legacy in the spring of 2008. For Smarty, the babies will take to the track in 2008 with great expectations riding on their backs. In a recent poll 43% of those asked wished to see Smarty Jones's foals more than any others. It will be interesting to watch the next generation strive to fill the horse shoes of these greats.

Part of Smarty's legacy is his calling to be an ambassador of sorts for thoroughbred racing. He may have lost his final race but his legend continues to grow. In Pennsylvania alone Smarty has helped to focus attention on the wonderful horse tradition. Many in the Philadelphia area have been touched by Smarty's magic. One such person was Gary Wills, who shared his story:

I had always dreamed that someday I would own my own horses. It wasn't until Smarty Jones captured our imagination that I decided to pursue that dream. Since then, I have been extremely involved in the horse-racing industry and am in the process of building my dream farm.

In speaking with Wayne Spillove, Pennsylvania Chairman of Museums, a horse museum is on a "wish list." "It would be wonderful to have one that would showcase the rich state history in breeding, racing, hunting and jumping."

At the time of Smarty's debut, thoroughbred racing was dealing with serious decline and looking for a way to reinvent itself. Some strides have been made in this regard and others will take more honest assessment and serious change. This journey can be made but it will have to be "one step at a time."

Back in 1992, presidential candidate Bill Clinton focused on one single issue which helped to get him elected. It became a catch phrase, "It's about the economy, stupid." This was hammered over the months and by November had made enough of an impression that he won the White House. In a *Blood-Horse* article, Sarah Reschly makes a great comparison, "It's about the horse, stupid." The public looks to racing to treat horses in a humane fashion. They want to see other Barbaros and Ruffians which will not be sacrificed on racetracks when they are hurt or past their prime. If conditions do not improve, the public will not support the sport as they had in the past. Other sports are pouring dollars in PR campaigns and fan incentives as they struggle for their market share. Professional sports' seasons are overlapping like never before and it is becoming an all-out effort to attract and maintain a consistent fan base. The question is, "Will thoroughbred racing have a fighting chance against these other formidable competitors?"

Ferdinand and Exceller

The most prestigious contest in all of thoroughbred racing, the Kentucky Derby, was won by a horse named Ferdinand in 1986. The following year at the age of four, Ferdinand captured four more stakes victories including the Hollywood Gold Cup and the Breeders' Cup Classic. For this excellence on the racetrack, he was voted the 1987 Horse of the Year, a most coveted award. By the time of his retirement in 1989, Ferdinand had earned $3,777,978 and was the fifth leading money winner of all time.

After the racetrack accolades had passed, Ferdinand moved on to a stud career as a breeding stallion at the renowned Claiborne Farm. By the fall of 1994 Ferdinand was sold to a Japanese breeding operation. At that time, the Japanese were aggressively seeking select American and European breeding stock and Ferdinand was a worthy addition to their stallion register.

When efforts in this country to locate Ferdinand failed in 2002, reporter Barbara Bayer pressed authorities to allow her to see the horse. It was only at this point that she learned that a Japanese horse dealer named Watanabe had taken the horse and disposed of him without contacting the original owners, the Keck family or Claiborne Farm. As Bayer wrote in *The Blood-Horse*, "No one can say for sure when and where Ferdinand met his end, but it would seem clear he met it in a slaughterhouse....In a country where racing is kept booming by the world's highest purses and astronomical betting revenues, Ferdinand's fate is not the exception. It is the rule." There are many breeding operations in Japan that would probably never endorse what happened to Ferdinand. Those things happen in the United States, too—it's about responsibility.

Another champion of the racetrack was Exceller. Born in France in 1973, Exceller won some important races as a three-year old before coming to this country in 1977. By 1978 Exceller had begun to make his mark in the U.S. by winning the Hollywood Gold Cup. He went on to win the Jockey Club Gold Cup in which he defeated two Triple Crown winners, Seattle Slew (1977) and Affirmed (1978). By the end of that year he had won seven out of ten races and earned $879,790.

In 1979 he was retired to stud at Gainesway Farm but over time was not very successful as a breeding stallion. By 1991 he had been sold to a Swedish breeder named Gote Ostlund. When nominated to the Thoroughbred racing Hall of Fame in 1997 Exceller once again became a topic of conversation, and reporter Mike Mullaney went in search of the horse's current whereabouts. At that point Mullaney made a ghastly discovery. Exceller had been killed because he was perceived to be a liability to his owner. The horse had not been ill or injured but on April 7, 1997 had been sent to a Swedish slaughterhouse.

With Exceller's death in 1997 the Thoroughbred racing industry needed to take inventory of previous horses which had passed from its sight. The death of Ferdinand struck an equally-sensitive nerve and signaled an alarm for greater accountability. A *Blood-Horse* article of 2003 related,

The death of Exceller in 1997 became the defining moment in the advent of Thoroughbred retirement farms throughout the United States to care for those horses who, in a thousand different ways, slip through the cracks when their primary career becomes yesterday's news.

As a direct result of Ferdinand and Exceller's deaths, many horse rescue operations have sprung up all across the country. Charities and retirement farms have increased considerably and clauses have been added to contracts, where owners seek to buy horses back at the end of their careers. In New York, the New York Thoroughbred Horsemen's Association and the New York Racing Association have created the Ferdinand Fee, which is a voluntary $2.00 fee for owners and horsemen desiring to make a donation. The proceeds are directed to ending the slaughter of horses in the United States. As the president of NYTHA, Richard Bomze explained, "This is a simple way to help horses and to end slaughter. We're going full speed ahead." Ferdinand Fee founder, Bill Heller added, "By working together, the New York racing industry has confronted the most important issue ever facing horses in America–their right to not be brutally slaughtered."

There are many horses that may no longer have quality of life or do not have anyone to take proper care of them. If there should not be a place for them within the confines of a retirement charity, they have a right to be humanely euthanized. Horse slaughter is not about keeping thousands of horses, which no longer have caregivers or sanctuaries. The debate is about outlawing the cruelty and brutality which accompany slaughtering. In the United States, there are three horse slaughtering plants–two in Texas and one in Illinois–as of January 2008 these have been closed. All three are foreign-owned; however, the facilities are under the jurisdiction of the United States Government in so far as their modes of operation.

The newly-formed National Horse Protection Coalition has named Hall of Fame trainer Nick Zito as its spokesperson. Zito has been one of the most vocal and effective proponents against horse slaughter in the United States. The purpose of this coalition is "to educate the American public on the topic of horse slaughter while working to ensure the passage of the American Horse Slaughter Prevention Act legislation." Zito announced,

It's a national tragedy that we've even had to form this coalition...I know that Ferdinand, the horses killed last year, those who will die this year and next year, deserve better treatment. I am dedicated to stopping this practice.

At many levels within the industry, people are trying to educate the masses and affect some kind of positive change. As Anne Peters at Three Chimneys Farm clearly explained,

Antislaughter is not about keeping horses, and especially old or infirmed horses, alive longer than they should be. It's about ridding them of the horrible physical, mental and psychological torture of the slaughter-houses....The issue is about brutality and responsibility.

Many Americans today are ignorant of the fate of these many unwanted horses in the United States. The Humane Society of the United States on its website and in its brochures outlines the specifics associated with this cruel and inhumane experience. Specifics address: painful and sometimes fatal modes of transportation, lack of food or water for days prior to slaughter, and grotesque methods of killing these horses. It is only by informing a vocal and moral public that practices such as these may be discontinued.

Horse Rescue

As efforts within the United States are focusing on Anti-Slaughter Legislation to protect thousands of old, infirmed or unwanted horses, another question remains. "What is the most humane and effective way to manage the large numbers of unwanted horses of every possible description?" Many of these horses are cast-offs from racing–horses that no longer perform at the desired level but others are non-racing horses or displaced horses. In some instances, a responsible breeder may sell a horse and lose track of that horse as the years pass. Within recent days, a half-brother of Secretariat at the age of thirty-two was intercepted on his way to slaughter.

At the time of this writing, all of the three foreign-owned slaughter houses in the United States have been shut down. Efforts are being directed to halting the shipping of these targeted horses to Canada or Mexico. The passing of the appropriate legislation in the United States can keep our horses here. Over-population will need to be dealt with through united efforts on all fronts. We see this trend existent among small animals, which may be feral and free to breed at will. In horse circles, most of these animals had a very real past but are laboring now with a very uncertain present and an even more questionable future.

Within North America, there are many different types of horse rescue groups. Some of these are individuals who attend auctions and buy horses that are being targeted by "Kill" buyers. Others accept, care for and place horses that have previously been rescued by another operation. By design, some groups are prepared to rehabilitate horses and direct them toward a second career–e.g. racing to show jumping. Other organizations may be fortunate enough to have the land needed for long-term retirement. In other instances, horses may be severely injured and may be beyond rehabilitation. Some walk around with serious injuries for months and even years. As one can see, the needs are great, the helping hands may be few and the needed resources even less.

One national adoption group, ReRun Inc. has developed what they call the "stickers program." When a foal or horse is registered with the Jockey Club, a sticker is placed on the back of that horse's certificate designating the group or individual to be contacted at the time of the animal's retirement. The tattoo under the horse's lip is the key identification link but the sticker enables that horse to have a future. The entire endeavor is about responsibility—breeder and owner. As Lori Neagle, former Chapter Director of ReRun Kentucky, explained,

Thoroughbreds can pass through multiple hands throughout their racing careers and are at risk when they are no longer productive as racehorses. These stickers provide a safety net for horses whose owners want to help them later on when it may be needed.

Even a sticker does not guarantee anything for the horse if the person holding the animal does not pursue it. It is a beginning and with greater education can make a difference. Through a national mailing Kim Zito and Carol Farmer are seeking to provide awareness and greater responsibility.

A newly-opened Kentucky Equine Humane Center is seeking to provide a variety of services for unwanted horses on its 85 acre leased property near Nicholasville, Kentucky. The center seeks to provide shelter and care for unwanted horses and to facilitate adoptions. All horses regardless of breed are assisted in whatever way possible; no one is turned away. The board of the newly- established center lists many prominent names in and out of the horse world. It is hoped that this effort will spur others to follow their lead with comparable settings and programs. Significant fund-raising efforts have been done to educate the public, as well as generate the needed resources to make a difference in the lives of many horses .In addressing the need for changes within the industry, Staci Hancock commented,

I think that we need to put more of "THE HORSE" back into the horse industry. Without a good healthy horse, we will not have a good healthy horse business. So I think that horse welfare, both individually and collectively, should come first. I wish that we would lower our supply of horses to fit the demand, take care of the horses we have on the ground with safer conditions and without performance-enhancing medication, and stop the mass slaughter of the ones who no longer meet our needs. Simply, there would be no horse industry without the horse and we need to do a better job of taking care of him and putting him first.

Several years ago in the *Blood-Horse* magazine, there was a very pointed article, entitled "Finding Alternatives," by Reiley McDonald. The message was so appropriate that it could have been penned yesterday–"address the dark existence and subsequent ending that these animals often encounter." Many of the good rescue efforts are being maxed out; they are successful, but they can only do so much. Organizations such as ReRun, New Vocations and even the Thoroughbred Retirement Foundation have been successful, but space is limited and there are so many other horses which need help. When it comes down to it, so much is about personal responsibility. As McDonald echoed,

> We must take care of the animals in our lives that provide us incredible sport. We need larger rehabilitation facilities designed to heal and re-train horses to a point where they can be competitive in other equine performance activities....There is an alternative to running their horses into the ground until they are chronically unsound and useless for any other purpose. Give your horse a chance.

On a final note, Dr. Tom Lenz recently wrote an article, "Commentary: Own Responsibly," for the *Blood-Horse*. The essence of his message is a much needed one. As the new chairman of the Unwanted Horse Coalition, he sets forth their mission: "to reduce the number of unwanted horses and to improve their welfare through education and the efforts of organizations committed to the health, safety, and responsible care and disposition of these horses."

The number of associations joining in is more than commendable and the specific groups are impressive. Efforts will be directed toward educating prospective owners before they purchase, and current owners before they breed and sell. A very detailed website links users to appropriate documents, which include: the plight of the unwanted horse, rescue and retirement, ownership, charitable organizations and euthanasia.

On the alexbrownracing.com website there are many rescue groups of every size and definition. Most states are included within the list and there are contact persons wherever possible. Little by little, things are being done to lessen the plight of these less fortunate ones. It is only by more people in the industry reaching out to help that effective change can be made. For those who already have horses, the only difference will come from taking a hold of the reins of responsibility–one horse at a time.

Track Surfaces

In a recent article entitled "Equine Safety Essential to Ensuring Fan Confidence," Ed DeRosa examined the need for a confidence boost for the public from the industry with respect to the safety of our fragile equine athletes. This was only one of many relevant topics discussed at the Thoroughbred Racing Association's International Simulcast Conference last fall in Philadelphia. People have become much more interested in the sport since the Triple Crown bids of Smarty Jones, Afleet Alex and Barbaro, yet these heroes are no longer racing due to life-ending or career-ending injuries. The two points up for serious consideration include: "Why are these injuries happening so frequently?" And secondly, "What is being done to turn this horrible tide of losing horses?"

For many, Barbaro was a wake-up call and a very late-coming one at that. What about Ruffian, Go For Wand and many others? It is unrealistic to pretend that injuries will not exist, for horses are actually 1200 pound muscled athletes running at thirty-five to forty miles per hour on toothpick legs. At this level, any fall, collision or misstep can bring the worst of scenarios to animals, whose legs are thin, poorly muscled and with minimal blood supply. Dick Jerardi, a turf writer for *The Philadelphia Daily News*, raised a valid point at the conference, "The public doesn't understand why these things happen; they are confused more than anything." All aspects of Barbaro's surgeries and care were shared with the general public on a daily basis, and that educational piece helped with the understanding of the post-injury picture. From a prevention standpoint, what will help the public to recognize progress in safety efforts?

Turfway President, Bob Elliston posed the big question, "What is racing doing about safety in the wake of Barbaro and breakdowns on the racetrack?" One of the answers to this question is the approval and installation of synthetic surfaces at racetracks. Michael Dickinson, horse trainer, invented one form called Tapeta Footings which many tracks have already begun to use. As he explained, "The industry had taken a blind eye to safety issues but no longer. If it had moved any slower [on safety issues], then it would have moved backwards."

Current proponents of these artificial/synthetic surfaces claim that horses working and training on these surfaces will be able to race more and more. The basic compositions seem to be more forgiving to the elements and permit easier maintenance. The Tapeta surface is a mixture of wax-coated sand, rubber and other fibers. Another form of synthetic surface is Polytrack; it contains silica sand, fibers and recycled materials. It is then covered with a wax coating, which permits the water to drain down vertically and allows the track to maintain a consistent depth. A third form is called Cushion Track. It is a mixture of silica sand mixed with synthetic fibers, elastic fiber and granulated rubber. The most recent form discussed is Safetrack, which is similar to Polytrack and Cushion Track. Safetrack is a synthetic all weather, fiber-enhanced surface, which also uses elastic on a different kind of base. All of the mixtures are ultimately covered with a blend of wax, but vertical channels allow for better drainage. It is hoped that all of the surfaces will provide consistency and resilience.

To date California is the only state that has mandated the use of synthetic surfaces by 2008. While many of the more prominent tracks have adopted synthetic surfaces, many are being more cautious for a variety of reasons. These include: 1) lack of documented evidence to support the reduction of injuries, 2) the cost of installation as an astronomical investment and 3) a long history of dirt pedigrees and dirt running. The next year or so will undoubtedly provide more relevant data to fuel future surface decisions.

Another effort toward greater safety is being generated by an associate professor of mechanical engineering at the University of Maine. From his research, Michael Peterson believes that certain types of track surfaces are contributing to an increase in hind leg breakdowns. He has invented a device that may be attached to a sports utility vehicle. As Peterson explained to *The Thoroughbred Times*, it will "measure track's stiffness and resistance by simulating the force of a Thoroughbreds hoof at full speed against the surface. An additional machine he developed uses ground radar to evaluate racetrack levelness and base." While Peterson's efforts are in the infant stages, any pertinent data related to greater safety will find a very receptive audience.

In the United States, racing is done on different surfaces: dirt, turf (grass) and synthetic. Most racing in Asia and Europe takes place on turf, and not the same quality that we may associative with a well-maintained park or well-manicured golf course. Horses are generally trained in facilities and not racetracks. Part of a horse's daily workout may include negotiating rugged and uneven ground, which older trainers and some younger would insist strengthens and develops bones in a better way. In discussion with Anne Peters at Three Chimneys Farm on this very subject, this author introduced the topic of the longer and more challenging careers of horses like Citation and Whirlaway. Anne remarked,

They [the Joneses, their trainers] trained differently and that is a symptom of why our horses do not appear as sound today. My belief is that they are not as well conditioned as the horses of the past were....those horses of the '40s had bottom (a solid foundation) on them. They have done studies that have proven if you don't really work a horse as a two-year-old, they don't have the same bone density as horses that are worked early. Many trainers err on the side of caution, and they are not really doing the horses any favor by being gentle with them. You have to stress the bones to make them hard, not abuse them, but some stress is required for the remodeling of the hard tissue in the legs. If you don't do that, then they are more fragile.

These differences in training are driven by different expectations on the racetrack. In some respects, one may draw the conclusion that there are two different sports out there–the one obsessed with the stopwatch and the other searching for stamina. In this country the emphasis is on bursts of speed, where in Europe the races are longer over rolling turf courses. The bottom line is that Europe and Asia experience fewer racetrack breakdowns–in the USA 1.5 per 1000 starts, Hong Kong .58 per 1000 starts and UK .65 per 1000 starts.

Over the next few years discussions concerning track surfaces will continue and additional research can only improve a rapidly-growing data base of information. In the wake of Barbaro's horrific injury, this author questioned Dr. Dean Richardson about his thoughts on the newly-introduced synthetic surfaces.

I think with repetitive stress injuries, it could end up making a difference....I think that it has huge potential, but like many things in the media, people are running away with it. Unless it's a proven fact, we don't know if it's going to diminish the injury rate with Thoroughbred race horses, and we don't know which injuries it's going to decrease....until it's proven by epidemiological studies that there is a difference, then it's still a work in progress....The thing for people to keep in mind, in my opinion, is that you still have a four or five hundred kilogram horse running at forty miles per hour. That is still an enormous amount of load; it's not going to make it all go away.

Fans of Barbaro

When the timwoolleyracing.com website (now alexbrownracing.com) was initiated, no one would have believed how extensive the audience would become. It would attract from all over the world, and become a tremendous force for good. What started out so simply became the "Barbaro information site" for months and months, and later a central meeting place for gathering thousands of folks, from all over the world, to affect change and to initiate better lives for horses.

Many of the followers watched Barbaro in his maiden race at Delaware Park or in the Laurel Futurity in Laurel, Maryland. As his popularity grew, so did his following. After his dramatic victory in the Kentucky Derby, the number swelled even more. Through his terrible misstep in the Preakness Stakes, on May 20, 2006, Barbaro became the focus of international attention which would continue beyond his death in January 2007. More fans joined the F.O.B.s at this stage through the numerous local and regional newspapers that listed the timwoolleyracing.com conduit.

The official F.O.B. webmaster, Alex Brown, formerly an exercise rider with Tim Woolley at Fair Hill Training Center in Maryland, is English-born. In his role with the website (now alexbrownracing.com), he has become the official contact person and spokesperson for the group. Major newspapers, magazines and TV stations work with Alex on a daily basis and the website has become a centerpiece for "all things horse." The activities of the F.O.B.s are reported almost hourly and emergency situations requiring immediate interventions are filtered to all parts of the country within minutes. Huge numbers of horses have been rescued and treated in their eleventh hour through the efforts of the F.O.B.s. The F.O.B.s describe themselves as,

> a passionate and unified group of people from all walks of life...The Fans of Barbaro are as close as your nearest computer. We hail from coast-to-coast in the U.S. and Canada, across the seas in Europe, the U.K., Australia, South Africa and beyond....In the name of Barbaro, we work to bring awareness and thereby resolve to all issues affecting the health and welfare of horses from all walks of life.

Over the last year, the F.O.B.s have made a presence in this country in Barbaro's name. There are special projects, which they are willing to support, in addition to the many desperate needs that surround horse welfare. As Debra Cline, an FOB, explained to this author at Barbaro's birthday celebration on April 29, 2007, "I think that even months after his departure from us, that he is still inside of us, stronger than ever, urging everyone of us to carry his legacy on in life." Some of their areas of special emphasis include: anti-slaughter legislation, horse rescue, horse retirement, safer racetrack surfaces/conditions and equine medical research. On the website there are numerous links to outreach groups which support all aspects of these critical areas.

A fund-raising effort and birthday celebration were held during the weekend of April 27, 2007 at Delaware Park, the site of Barbaro's maiden race. Through Friday and Saturday evenings, over $20,000 was raised for Thoroughbred

Charities of America to assist in all areas of need. On Sunday there was a spirited cook-out attended by over 500 F.O.B.s from all over the world. Mr. and Mrs. Jackson visited the F.O.B.s, addressed pertinent topics and signed autographs for the assembled group. All of the major newspapers and TV stations were represented, as well as significant persons from different aspects of Barbaro's life and care. Earlier that day there had been an Open House at Fair Hill Training Center, the barn of Barbaro's trainer Michael Matz. Many attended the event and tour. Speaking at the Delaware Park Birthday Celebration were: Dr. Kathy Anderson (Barbaro's regular veterinarian), Dr. Corinne Sweeney (Dean of New Bolton Center, of the University of Pennsylvania School of Veterinary Medicine), Ms. Jeanine Edwards (ESPN), Tim Woolley (horse trainer and website sponsor), Mike Rea (disabled jockey from Fair Hill) and Eduardo (Barbaro's groom). Using that event as a catalyst, many F.O.B. groups have planned similar events within their local areas. All details are presented on the website.

Reflection

In our engagement with these horses we have allowed ourselves to be vulnerable. Anything of real merit or value always has a price tag attached, and some are far more costly than others. In a *Washington Post* article entitled *Bottomless Heart*, Sally Jenkins attempted to examine why Barbaro engaged the American public to the degree that he did. For Jenkins it came down to his innocence and greatness. This author wishes to take it one step further. All of these horses were innocent and great and they were vulnerable. They gave one hundred percent to that which they did well. They were aware of the public's attention and adulation, and they sought humankind and relished the interaction. While all of this is true, there is a stronger message than these. The feelings, attitudes and sentiments which they engendered in others are something that brought their greatness to another level. In today's world, we see little of true giving without the cost being measured. There are always clauses and risks attached. These horses, in their simplicity and benevolence, seemed to bring out the goodness in people. People gave and called and wrote and prayed when Barbaro had his tragic accident. The outpouring was beyond what anyone had seen in a very long time. A similar situation occurred with Ruffian; however, her life was short-lived after her injury. For Smarty, people still make pilgrimages to see him, they write to him and they celebrate his legacy. We are better for having had them pass through our lives.

Anyone who watched Smarty's retirement, Barbaro's convalescence or Ruffian's injury will attest to the wonderful care which they received. With ownership goes a corresponding responsibility. They are innocent animals that depend on us for all of their needs to be met. With this ownership comes untold hours of enjoyment and pleasure. The goodness, which Ruffian, Smarty and Barbaro have brought out in each one of us, should help to make the world a better place to be...even if it is by one small step at a time. For the less fortunate horses, the displaced horses, the injured horses and the homeless horses... let today be a beginning for others because of the great legacy which they have left to each of us.

Glossary

The Horse

Broodmare – a female horse for breeding only

Colt – a non-castrated male horse through his 4th year

Dam – a horse's mother

Filly – a female horse up to her 4th year

Foal – a horse under the age of 1 year (January 1 serves as the official birthday for all horses)

Gait – the manner in which a horse moves its legs (e.g. gallop, canter, pace, trot, etc.)

Gallop – the fastest of all gaits

Gelding – a male horse that has been castrated

Juvenile – a horse that is two-years old

Mare – a female horse in her 5th year or older

Pace – a two-beat gait, where the two legs on the same side of the body move forward at the same time. (Faster than a trot)

Sire – a horse's father

Stallion – an uncastrated male horse over the age of four

Standardbred – a hardy American hybrid of the Thoroughbred and other hardy strains-(generally used for harness racing)

Stud – a breeding stallion

Thoroughbred – a horse that comes from the original foundation sires, the Byerly Turk, the Godolphin Arabian and the Darley Arabian.

Trot – a two-beat gait in which the front leg on one side of the horse's body moves forward with the hind leg on the other side of the body

Two-year old – a horse after January 1st of its 2nd year (eligible for racing)

Weanling – a young foal at the point when it is separated from its mother; usually the fall of its 1st year

Yearling – the horse after it passes its first January 1

Colors

Bay – a variation of brown, moving from a light tan to a dark mahogany; all bays exhibit black points (mane, tail, forelock and lower legs)

Black – a true black horse generally has fine black hair on its muzzle, no light areas

Brown – very similar to bay, dark bay or black; a brown horse generally has tan/brown hairs on flanks or face

Chestnut – variations exist from yellow to brilliant red to copper or liver color; a chestnut may have light points (mane, tail, forelock and lower legs)

Gray – a progressive combination of black and white hairs; many black foals will lighten over time to gray

Roan – a gray color consistent from birth, head and legs devoid of white hair, many will contain chestnut hairs

Horse Ailments

Bleeder – some horses may have nasal bleeding or mouth hemorrhaging due to respiratory strain

Breaking Down – when a horse goes lame; it is generally due to an ailment or injury

Laminitis – an inflammation of the laminae within the horse's hoof which causes separation of the hoof from the coffin bone

Osselets – boney arthritic growth in a swollen ankle joint area (fetlock); in many instances both front ankles may be affected

Splint – an inflamed swollen separation on a horse's splint bone (along the insides of the cannon bone and not the outside)

At the Track

Also ran – a horse finishing a race that does not earn win, place or show (did not finish in the money)

Apprentice – an inexperienced beginner jockey

Backstretch – a straightaway area on the non-commercial side of the racetrack, the barn area

Blinkers – eye cups (approved by racing stewards) that modify the visual path of the horse for a variety of reasons; some block and others focus

Breezing – working a horse at a moderate speed

Claiming Race – a horse placed in a claming race is offered for purchase; prospective owners must initiate the claim prior to the running of the race. ($1,000 is the minimum price)

Clocker – an individual who identifies horses and times their morning workouts within fractions of seconds; it is imperative that the identity of each horse is confirmed at the time of the clocking

Dead Heat – when 2 or more horses are tied for the win; a photo finish reflects the horses' heads in exactly the same position with respect to the finish line

Eighth Pole – a pole 1/8th of a mile before the finish line

Entry – two or more horses of the same owner or trainer participating in the same race. The horses are generally given the same number with letters as subdivisions; e.g. 1 and 1A. All or both of the horses are considered a single betting unit.

Also, a horse that qualifies to run in a race.

Furlong – originally an agricultural term, the length of a plowed field, which translates to our 1/8ᵗʰ of a mile; 220 yards

Hand – a unit of measure equal to four inches. A horse's height is generally measured by placing one hand on top of the other from the ground to the withers (saddle seat.)

Handily – a horse going easily to win a race with no prompting from the jockey

Home stretch – the portion of the track directly before and leading up to the finish line.

Infield – all of the land within the inner rail at the center of the racetrack

Irons – the stirrups on the saddle

Maiden Race – horses participating in this race have not previously won in a formal racing meet; for the horse that wins, it has broken its maiden.

Odds-On – odds of less than even money.

Outriders – additional horses and riders that have many functions: leading horses to the starting gate, assisting injured horses and capturing runaway horses.

Paddock – an area at the racetrack where horses are saddled for a race and bettors gather to view the horses.

Pari-Mutual – betting which assigns odds to the particular horses based on wagered money; a French meaning for "bet among us"

Post – where the race begins, location of the starting gate; starting point of the race

Quarter Pole – one quarter of a mile before the finish line

Racing Secretary – a racing official, who determines the terms of the race, and in handicap races, assigns the weight; also, the person in charge of the operation and organization of the racetrack

Scratch – when a horse is withdrawn from a race after the closing of entry

Sex Allowance – in every race, horses carry specific weight allowances. Mares and 3-4 year old fillies carry 5 fewer pounds, than colts, geldings or stallions. Two-year-old fillies carry 2 fewer pounds.

Silks – the brightly colored jacket and cap worn by a jockey. Each owner designs his/her particular colors and patterns, which must be registered with the appropriate authorities. These colors and patterns assist spectators and racing authorities in distinguishing among horses in a race.

Starter – the person who begins the race by pressing the button to open the stall door, when all horses and jockeys are poised and ready

Stayer – a horse that runs well for long distances

Steward – one who presides over the race meet (consecutive racing days), a racing official who is responsible for monitoring the actual race for ethical and appropriate behavior; should it be necessary, any disqualifications, suspensions, hearings or disciplinary action would be initiated and overseen by the steward

Timer (**electronic**) – a device that times all parts of the race, and displays all times on the race board

Timer –an individual who times the entire race and posts on the race board all of the times at different intervals during the race; times are also recorded for the horses within fractions of seconds

Index

Bibliography

Alter, A. (1982). *Champions: Amazing race horses.* Morristown, NJ: Contemporary Perspectives, Inc.

Claflin, E. (1975). *Ruffian: Queen of the fillies.* New Canaan, CT: Scrambling Press.

Drager, M. (2005). *The most glorious crown.* Chicago: Triumph Books.

Georgeff, P. (2003). *Citation: In a class by himself.* New York: Taylor Trade Publishing.

Heller, B. (2006). *Saratoga tales: Great horses, fearless jockeys, shocking upsets and incredible blunders at America's legendary race track.* Albany, NY: Whitston Publishing Company, Inc.

Hillenbrand, L. (2001). *Seabiscuit: An American legend.* New York: Ballantine Books.

Jones, W. DVM, PhD. (1992). *Sports medicine for the racehorse.* Wildomar, CA: Veterinary Data.

Lifshin, L. (2005). *The Licorice daughter: My year with Ruffian.* Huntsville, TX: Texas Review Press.

Marr, C. (1999). *Cardiology of the horse.* New York: W B Saunders.

Nack, W. (1975). *Secretariat: The making of a champion.* Cambridge, MA: Da Capo Press.

Philbin, T. & Brodowsky, P. (2007). *Barbaro: A nation's love story.* New York: HarperCollins Publishers.

Rachlis, E. & Lefcourt, B. (eds). 2001). *Horse racing: The golden age of the track.* San Francisco: Chronicle Books LLC.

Schwartz, J. (1991). *Ruffian: Burning from the start.* New York: The Random House Publishing Group.

Sports Publishing LLC. (2004). *Smarty Jones: America's horse.* Champaign, IL: Sports Publishing LLC.

Taylor, J. (1993). *Complete guide to breeding and raising racehorses.* Neenah, WI: The Russell Meerdink Company, Ltd.

The Blood-Horse (2005). *10 Best Kentucky derbies.* Lexington, KY: Eclipse Press.

The Blood-Horse (2006). *Horse racing's top 100 moments.* Lexington, KY: Eclipse Press.

Valentine, B. (2004). *Smarty Jones: Forever a champion.* Malibu, CA: Braveheart Press, LLC.

Ruffian–Periodicals

Associated Press (1975). *NYRA flag half staff for dead filly Ruffian*. Lexington Herald-Leader, July 9.

Associated Press (1975). *Doctor scorns theory of saving Ruffian*. Lexington Herald-Leader, July 10.

Bailey, L (1975). *Money from area youngsters pays for Ruffian memorial*. Daily Racing Form, December 1.

Bolus, J. (1990). *They do it the Whiteley way*. Keeneland, Spring-Summer, 5-23.

Bowen, E.L. (1978). *The hall of famer*. Blood-Horse, 5474-5486.

Cox, T. (1974). *Find Ruffian's measurements even overshadow Secretariat's*. Daily Racing Form, September 9.

Fitzpatrick, F. (2007). *Special bond makes final decision tough*. The Philadelphia Inquirer, January 30.

Graves, M. (1992). *Ruffian remembered in style*. The Times Union, D-6, April 22.

Harthill, A. (1975). *Ruffian twice revived from dead by various means in vain attempt to save filly champion*. Daily Racing Form, July 9.

Hicks, A. (1991). *Ruffian's sad story*. Gannett News Service, October 19.

Howley, J. (1995). *Ruffian remembered*. Equus *218*, 27-31.

Johnson, W. O. (1975). *Could she have been saved?* Sports Illustrated, July 21, 22-24.

Kelly, J. (1986). *Exercise rider Kennedy recalls Ruffian*. Daily Racing Form, March 8.

Kindred, D. (1975). *The lady ran out of luck*. Louisville Courier-Journal, July 7.

Lynch, P. (1988). *Vasquez memories of superfilly Ruffian*. October 6.

Lyon, B. (1974). *Ruffian's spirit cost her life*. Lexington Herald-Leader, July 8.

Mann, J. (1975). *It ended with one fatal step*. Sports Illustrated, July 14, 16-17.

Mann, J. (1975). *They'll burn from the start*. Sports Illustrated, July 7, 24-29.

Milbert, N. (1999). *Death of a beauty*. Lexington Herald-Leader, July 9, C-9.

Nack, W. (1975). *The Ruffian tragedy*. Horse and Rider, October, 17-23.

Nagler, B. (1975). *Ruffian's fate a terrible loss to horse racing*. Daily Racing Form, July 9.

Nichols, J. *Unbeaten Ruffian appears a shoo-in for no. 10 today*. The New York Times, June 21, 16.

Reed, B. (1975). *Chances were nil: Dr. Reed claims Ruffian couldn't have been saved*. Louisville Courier-Journal, July 23.

Reed, B. (2000). *Ruffian unmatched even after 25 years*. Lexington Herald-Leader.

Rudy, W. H. (1975). *Summons to a silent hall*. The Blood-Horse, July 14, 2712-2717.

Sandomir, R. (2006). *Breakdown echoes in broadcasts of past stumbles*. The New York Times, May 23.

Zamarelli, D. (1974). *A gold-plated Cadillac*. The Blood-Horse. August 4, 3102-3149.

Ruffian–Electronic Sources

Dulay, C. P. *Ruffian*. Retrieved from
   http://horseracing.about.com/library/pics/blruffian.htm

Grening, D. *ESPN wraps up the filming of Ruffian*. Retrieved from
   http://horseracing.sportsline.com/cbs/haedlines/showarticle.aspx?
   articleId=8350

Grening, D. *Great match race still haunts jockey*. Retrieved from
   http://espn.go.com/horse/news/2000/0705/619299.html

Harris, B. *Racehorse breakdowns pack emotional wallop*. Retrieved from
   http://www.gohorsebetting.com/racingarticle.php?id=839

Hegarty, M. *Ruffian remembered on espn classic*. Retrieved from
   http://sports.espn.go.com/sports/horse/news/story?id=610063

Jones, K. *Ruffian*. Retrieved from
   http://thoroughbredchampions.com/biographies/ruffian1.htm

Lifshin, L. *On the 30th anniversary of Ruffian's last race*. Retrieved from
   http://www.printthis.clickability.com/pt/cpt?action=cpt&title=
   On+the+30th+Anniversary+0...

O'Connor, J. Great horses in history: Ruffian. Retrieved from
   http://www.horseandhound.co.uk/competitionnews/359/56979.html

Rhoades, S. *Ruffian:* Perfection unmatched. Retrieved from
   http://hometown.aol.com/racehorses1000/championsRuffian1.html

Schmidt, N. *Racing is much different today than it used to be. The careers of t h o r -
oughbreds are shorter and theories why abound*. Retrieved from
   http://www.enquirer.com/editions/2004/05/01/spt_sptderby1horses.html

Schwartz, J. *Why even strangers love a horse*. Retrieved from
   http://www.sfgate.com/cgi-
bin/article.cgi?file=/c/a/2006/05/28/SPGORJ2G1I1.DTL&type..

Smith, G. *Ruffian.* Retrieved from
http://www.americanheritage.com/articles/magazine/ah/1993/5/1993
_5_46_print.shtml

Wikipedia. *Ruffian.* Retrieved from
http://en.wikipedia.org/wiki/Ruffian_(horse)

Zinoman, J. *Ruffian breaks her leg in racing's battle of the sexes.* Retrieved from
http://sport.guardian.co.uk/horseracing/osm/story/0,,1982024,00.html

Ruffian: What made her great made her die. Retrieved on January 28, 2000 from
http://www.reines-de-course.com/ruffian.htm

Could Ruffian have been saved? Retrieved on January 28, 2007 from
http://www.time.com/time/magazine/printout/0,8816,913296,00.html

In memory of Ruffian. Retrieved on January 28, 2007 from
http://www.chai-
online.org/en/compassion/entertainment_racing_ruffian.htm

Ruffian. Retrieved on January 28, 2007 from
http://www.racingmuseum.org/hall/horse.asp?ID=128

Famous horses: Ruffian. Retrieved on January 28, 2007 from
http://www.dannysheridan.com/horse-racing/fh-ruffian.php

Ruffian: The destruction of a masterpiece. Retrieved from January 28, 2007 from
http://www.manesandtailsorganization.org/ruffian_destruction_of_the
_masterpieces.htm

Ruffian. Retrieved on January 28, 2007 from
http://www.spiletta.com/UTHOF/ruffian.html

The great Ruffian. Retrieved on January 28, 2007 from
http://www.kolumbus.fi/Catrine/faktasidor/thegreatruffian.htm

Ruffian Blood-Horse Sources

(1975) pp.176, 1283, 1285, 1546, 1958, 2198, 2216, 2271, 2475, 2477, 2500, 2665, 2711, 2712, 2994, 5312, 5711; (1976) pp. 49, 338, 660, 3047, 334 (1977) pp. 5971; (1978) pp. 5484; (1979) pp. 2841; (1980) pp. 2071, 5664; (1981) pp. 6077, 6012, 2315; (1982) pp. 4092; (1989) pp. 2258; (1991) pp. 5844 (1992) pp. 2311; (1996) pp. 4660; (1997) pp. 4536; (1998) pp. 1270; (1999) pp. 1337, 1340; (2000) pp. 3829, 3847, 3906, 4018, 4118, 4274, 4396; (2005) pp. 3714, 4430; (2006) pp. 552.

Smarty Jones-Periodicals

Alber, W. (2004). *NYRA awaits huge turnout for Smarty's Triple Crown bid.* Thoroughbred Times, May 22.

Beech, M. (2004). *Horse sense: Those who still doubt Smarty Jones would be wise to reconsider.* Sports Illustrated, May 8.

Beech, M. (2004). *Smarty's over.* Sports Illustrated, August 9.

Blackford, L. (2006). *Smarty Jones' new title: America's painter (sort of).* Philadelphia Inquirer, January 8.

Bozich, R. (2005). *America's still crazy about Smarty.* The Louisville-Courier Journal, May 1.

Donnelly, C. (2004). *Nothing but love for Smarty.* Philadelphia Inquirer, August 3.

Donnelly, C. (2004). *Hometown crowd picked the smart choice to win.* Philadelphia Inquirer, May 16.

Fitzpatrick, F. (2004). *Fate stepped in for Smarty-even before birth.* Philadelphia Inquirer, May 26.

Fitzpatrick, F. (2004). *Saddled with questions.* Philadelphia Inquirer, June 3.

Ford, B. (2004). *The only sure thing: A great time for fans.* Philadelphia Inquirer, May 1.

Ford, B. (2004). *Smarty Jones one step from ultimate glory.* Philadelphia Inquirer, June 2.

Ford, B. (2004). *Smarty's trainer lingers with ghosts of Derby lore.* Philadelphia Inquirer, May 2.

Ford, B. (2004). *Rags-to-roses rider takes it all in stride.* Philadelphia Inquirer, May 2.

Gildea, W. (2004). *Smarty Jones retired from racing.* Washington Post, August 3.

Jensen, M. (2004). *Ex-farm boss was there from the foaling.* Philadelphia Inquirer, May 27.

Jensen, M. (2004). *Champing at the bit to root for Smarty Jones.* Philadelphia Inquirer, May 1.

Jensen, M. (2004). *Secretariat's jockey rooting for Smarty.* Philadelphia Inquirer, June 4.

Jensen, M. (2004). *Champ returns to relax before seeking Triple Crown.* Philadelphia Inquirer, May 17.

Jensen, M. (2004). *Pace scenarios put Belmont burden on jockey.* Philadelphia Inquirer, June 2.

Jensen, M. (2004). *It's Smarty Jones's team all the way.* Philadelphia Inquirer, June 2.

Jensen, M. (2004). *Smarty Jones streaks to an 11-1/2-length victory.* Philadelphia Inquirer, May 15.

Jensen, M. (2004). *One colt, many dreams.* Philadelphia Inquirer, May 15.

Jensen, M. (2004). *Smarty's burden is bigger than ever.* Philadelphia Inquirer, May 15.

Jensen, M. (2004). *Noteworthy doubter joins ranks of Smarty Jones cnverts.* Philadelphia Inquirer, May 18.

Jensen, M. (2004). *Memories of Smarty's slain trainer remain alive.* Philadelphia Inquirer, May 17.

Jensen, M. (2004). *$100,000 per mare for Smarty.* Philadelphia Inquirer, September 10.

Jensen, M. (2004). *Smarty sits pretty.* Philadelphia Inquirer, May 14.

Jensen, M. (2004). *Team Smarty feels butterflies.* Philadelphia Inquirer, June 4.

Jensen, M. (2004). *Smarty Jones put out to stud as racing career ends.* Philadelphia Inquirer, August 3.

Jensen, M. & Donnelly, C. (2004). *Smarty Jones's run to greatness ends.* Philadelphia Inquirer, August 3.

Jensen, M. & Donnelly, C. (2004). *Smarty's a scratch for Pa. Derby.* Philadelphia Inquirer, July 27.

Jensen, M. (2004). *Colt is tested at 7 furlongs with fastest speed at end.* Philadelphia Inquirer, May 29.

Jensen, M. (2004). *Smarty Jones arrives in N. Y., draws outside position.* Philadelphia Inquirer, June 3.

Jensen, M. & Donnelly, C. (2004). *Smarty passes test en route to Preakness.* Philadelphia Inquirer, May 8.

Jensen, M. (2004). *Dreams, schemes and other extremes.* Philadelphia Inquirer, June 4.

Jensen, M. (2004). *Philly's Smarty Jones dazzles at the Derby.* Philadelphia Inquirer, May 2.

Law, T. (2004). *Ah oh so Smarty way to win.* Thoroughbred Times, May 8.

Law, T. (200). *Out for more than respect.* Thoroughbred Times, May 15.

Lelinwalla, M. (2004). *Residents appreciate horse's deep impact.* Philadelphia Inquirer, August 3.

Lyon, B. (2004). *The proper perspective on Smarty.* Philadelphia Inquirer, May 15.

Lyon, B. (2004). *Smarty looks even better now.* Philadelphia Inquirer, May 17.

Lyon, B. (2004). *Smarty Jones wins the Preakness.* Philadelphia Inquirer, May 16.

Lyon, B. (2004). *Elliott gets right back in the saddle.* Philadelphia Inquirer, May 4.

Lyon, B. (2004). *Three-track trek tests a horse's heart.* Philadelphia Inquirer, May 30.

Lyon, B. (2004). *Triple Crown eluded Smarty's reach.* Philadelphia Inquirer, June 6.

Lyon, B. (2004). *Big horse has big following.* Philadelphia Inquirer, May 9.

Lyon, B. (2004). *A triumphant return home.* Philadelphia Inquirer, May 4.

MacDonald, M. (2004). Pursuing *destiny–and a Triple Crown.* Thoroughbred Times, May 22.

Mooney, B. (2004). *Turning dreams into reality.* Thoroughbred Times, May 8.

Mooney, B. (2004). *Foes in awe after Smarty's party.* Thoroughbred Times, May 22.

Reed. B. (2004). *Rookie history favors a Triple Crown.* Thoroughbred Times, May 15.

Sheridan, P. (2004). *Too much at stake to keep champ racing.* Philadelphia Inquirer, August 3.

Sheridan, P. (2004). *Horse sense.* Philadelphia Inquirer, August 3.

Simon, M. (2004). *Jewels of Pennsylvania's crown.* Thoroughbred Times, May 15.

Smarty Jones: Heart of a Champion. Inter-County Newspaper Group, April 28, 2005.

Smith, P. (2004). *Record crowd beats the heat at Pimlico.* Thoroughbred Times, May 22.

Smith, S. (2004). *At Pimlico, a day of second chances.* Philadelphia Inquirer, May 16.

Snider, R. (2004). *Rivals unlikely to block Smarty.* The Washington Times, June 4.

Snider, R. (2004). *Nation ready to party hardy for Smarty.* The Washington Times, June 5.

Snider, R. (2004). *Smarty retired with minor injury.* The Washington Times, August 3.

Sparkman, J. (2004). *The wisdom of the deeper pedigree.* Thoroughbred Times, May 8.

Sparkman, J. (2004). *Blowout in Baltimore.* Thoroughbred Times, May 22.

Stable, A. (2004). *Holy sheets! Smarty's no lock.* New York Post, June 5.

Steinberg, D. (2004). *Chapman humor remains sharp.* Philadelphia Inquirer, May 16.

Steinberg, D. (2004). *Smarty's a four-legged money machine.* Philadelphia Inquirer, May 16.

Steinberg, D. (2004). *Major sponsors race to cash in on Smarty Jones.* Philadelphia Inquirer, May 26.

Steinberg, D. (2004). *Industry's fortunes may ride on Smarty's back.* Philadelphia Inquirer, June 4.

Steinberg, D. (2004). *Derby win raises parents' stock.* Philadelphia Inquirer, May 9.

Tanfani, J. (2004). *At last, Philly fans have a champion to cheer...the four-legged Smarty Jones.* Philadelphia Inquirer, May 2.

Wilson, A. (2006). *Smarty Jones now a father.* Philadelphia Inquirer, January 11.

Wincze, A. (2004). *Smarty's story captivates wide range of fans.* Thoroughbred Times, May 15.

Smarty Jones Blood-Horse Citations

(2004) pp. 1436, 2482, 2620, 2645, 2674, 2684, 2734, 2778, 2795, 2919, 2934, 2938, 2956, 3009, 3010, 3035,3094, 3106, 3109, 3111, 3135, 3194, 3239, 3264, 3266, 3277, 3278, 358, 3373, 3380, 3458, 3470, 3478, 3497, 3570, 3593, 3682, 3791, 4024, 4142, 4504, 4618, 4958, 4968, 4991, 5090, 5480, 6270, 6320, 6324, 6483, 6628, 6986,.

(2005) pp. 406, 766, 1113, 1515, 2898, 3990, 5747,

(2006) pp. 326, 369, 908, 1238, 5704, 5808.

Barbaro – Electronic Sources

Bailey, R. *5-week hiatus pays off for Matz*. Retrieved from
http://www.kentucky.com/mld/kentucky/sports/horse_racing/kentucky
_derby/145_19228...

Beyer, A. *In the mud, Barbaro wins holy bull*. Retrieved from
*http://www.washingtonpost.com/wp-
dyn/content/article/2006/02/04/AR2006020401144...*

Beyer, A. *With Barbaro, what could have been*. Retrieved from
http://www.msnbc.msn.com/id/16879908/print/1/displaymode/1098/

Biles, D. B. *Gretchen Jackson: It's still day to day, but Barbaro 'starting to blossom.'*
Retrieved from
http://news.bloodhorse.com/viewstory.asp?id=35269

Brown, K. S. (ed). *Thank you, Barbaro*. Retrieved from
http://www.thehorse.com/PrintArticle.aspx?ID=8802

Bredar, C. *Barbaro keeps record perfect, triumphs in holy bull stakes*.
Retrieved from
http://www.kentruckyderby.com/2006/derby_coverage/derby
_news/derby_news_0204200...

Cain, G. *After difficult birth, Barbaro thrived*. Retrieved from
http://www.ntra.com/content.aspx?type=news&id=17788

Chicoine, C. L. *A horse, a girl, and a crown that almost was*. Retrieved from
http://www.cst-phl.com/060608/seventh.html

Chicoine, C. L. *Highs and lows – derby winner's co-owner finds perspective in faith*.
Retrieved from
http://www.catholic.org/national/national_story.php?id=20496

CNN.com. *Vet: Barbaro was 'different horse' in final hours*. Retrieved from
http://cnn.usnews.printthis.clickability.com/pt/cpt?action=cpt&title
=Vet%3A+Barbaro+was...

Coffman, K. *Que Barbaro*. Retrieved from
http://www.highplainsmessenger.com/2006/05/que_barbaro.php

Curry, M. *Owner says amputation was never seriously considered for Barbaro.* Retrieved from
http://thoroughbredtimes.com/news/printable.aspx

Curry, M. *Profile on Lael farm.* Retrieved from
http://thoroughbredtimes.com/national-news/2007/February/01/Profile-on-Lael-Farm.aspx

Denk, P. *Richardson: Time was right to euthanize Barbaro.* Retrieved from
http://www.thoroughbredtimes.com/news/printable.aspx

Curry, M. & Denk, P. *Kentucky derby winner Barbaro euthanized.* Retrieved from
http://www.thoroughbredtimes.com/news/printable.aspx

Denk, P. & Curry, M. *Barbaro: April 29, 2006 – January 29, 2007.* Retrieved from
http://www.thoroughbredtimes.com/news/printable.aspx

Deford, F. *Sweetness and light.* Retrieved from
http://www.npr.org/templates/story.php?storyId=7381274&sc=emaf

Drape, J. *Barbaro's plight shined a light on advances.* Retrieved from
http://www.nytimes.com/2007/01/31/sports/othersports/31barbaro.html?_r=2&oref=slogin...

Drape, J. *With costly care, Barbaro's long odds improve.* Retrieved from
http://www.nytimes.com/2006/08/21/sports/othersports/21barbaro.html?ex=1313812800...

Engber, D. *Why a broken leg is bad news for a horse.* Retrieved from
http://www.slate.com/id/2142159/?nav=ais

Fine, S. *Thinking about Barbaro.* Retrieved from
http://www.mysummercamps.com/forum/For_Campers/Parents_C1/Camp_Scholar_F16/...

Ford, P. *Barbaro's death: Equine beauty meets harsh reality.* Retrieved from
http://sports.espn.go.com/sports/horse/colmuns/story?columnist-forde_pat&id=2747259

Gardner, K. *Going the distance – Barbaro reminded us that life is worth fighting for.* Retrieved from http://www.fredericknewsport.com/sections/storyTools/print_story.htm?storyID=56478&ca...

Grening, D. *Still in wonder of Barbaro's potential.* Retrieved from http://www.ntra.com/content.aspx?type=news&id=21532

Haskin, S. *Reflections on Barbaro and his fight for life.* Retrieved from http://www.bloodhorse.com.viewstory_plain.asp?id=37320

Haskin, S. *Racing analysis.* Retrieved from http://tcm.bloodhorse.com/BarbaroSpotlight.asp

Ireland, J. *Remembering Barbaro.* Retrieved from http://www.delawareonline.com/apps/pbcs.dll/article?Date=20070430&Category=NEWS...

Jenkins, S. *A 'bottomless' heart.* Retrieved from http://www.washingtonpost.com/wp-dyn/content/article/2007/01/29/AR2007012902109.ht...

Jensen, M. *Barbaro makes it into the movies.* Retrieved from http://www.philly.com/mld/philly/16619652.htm?template=contentModules/printstory.jsp

Jensen, M. *Standing by Barbaro.* Retrieved from http://www.phillyu.com/mld/philly/news/special_packages/latest/15592399.htm

Jerardi, D. *Barbaro's spirit lives.* Retrieved from http://www.printthis.clickability.com/pt/cpt?action=cpt&title=Barbaro%27s+spirit+lives+...

McMullen, S. *A fight too far for champion.* Retrieved from http://www.sundayherald.com/misc/print.php?artid=1168436

McMurray, J. *Kentucky horsemen recall Barbaro's early day.* Retrieved from http://www.msnbc.msn.com/id/16908885/print/1/displaymode/1098/

Marroni, S. *Barbaro's painter recalls horse's strength.* Retrieved from
http://www.eveningsun.com.portlet/article/html/fragments/
print_article.jsp?articleId=51179...

Musgrave, T. *Letters from Barbaro fans.* Retrieved from
http://thoroughbredtimes.com/national-news/2007/
February/02/memories-of-barbaro.aspx

The New York Times. *One horse dies.* Retrieved from
http://www.nytimes.com/2007/01/30/opinions/30tue4.html?_r
=3&oref=slo.in&pagewanted...

Pedulla, T. *Against all odds, Barbaro perseveres.* Retrieved from
http://www.usatoday.com/sports/horses/2006-10-10-barbaro-cover-
story_x.htm

Plonk, J. *We'll always remember Barbaro's battle.* Retrieved from
http://msn.foxsports.com/horseracing/story/6421942?print=true

Privman, J. *Matz soldiers on with Barbaro gone.* Retrieved from
http://www.msnbc.msn.com/id/16909272/print/1/displaymode/1098/

Rosenblatt, R. *Barbaro's final home still undecided.* Retrieved from
http://hosted.ap.org/dynamic/stories/R/RAC_BARBARO-
DAY_AFTER?SITE=PAPIT&...

Rosenblatt, R. *Barbaro's legacy guaranteed to last.* Retrieved from
http://www.bloodhorse.com/viewstory_plain.asp?id=37404

Scheinman, J. *Barbaro is able to stand after surgery.* Retrieved from
http://www.washingtonpost.com/wp-
dyn/content/article/2006/05/21/AR2006052100441...

Shinar, J. *Barbaro breathes fire in winning holy bull.* Retrieved from
http://tcm.bloodhorse.com/viewstory.asp?id=32053

Sports Network. *Chalk it up to racing luck.* Retrieved from
http://www.nbc4.com/horseracing/9281653/detail.html

Sullivan, T. *Barbaro saga sheds light on racing industry.* Retrieved from
http://www.signonsandiego.com/sports/sullivan/
20060524-9999-1s24sullivan.html

Telias, B. *Pace will make the race Saturday in derby.* Retrieved from
http://www.sportingnews.com/experets/brad-telias/blog/735312.html

Torg, E. *Kentucky derby roses, Springside kudos for 'lifer.'* Retrieved from
http://www.chestnuthilllocal.com/issues/2006.05.18/locallife1.html

Twomey, S. *Barbaro's legacy.* Retrieved from
http://www.smithsonianmagazine.com/issues/2007/april/barbaro.htm

Welsch, M. *Barbaro still has much to prove.* Retrieved from
http://www.ntra.com/content.aspx?type=news&id=16997

Wesch, H. *Barbaro a tale of compassion.* Retrieved from
http://www.signonsandiego.com/sports/20060527-9999-1s27horsecol.html

Wikipedia. *Barbaro.* Retrieved from
http://en.wikipedia.org/wiki/Barbaro

Williams, T. *Fans gather to honor Barbaro on his birthday.* Retrieved from
http://wjz.com/sports/local_story_119174718.html

Zast, V. *Zast: Barbaro's impact, legacy to live on.* Retrieved from
http://www.msnbc.msn.com/id/16876039/print/1/displaymode/1098/

Associated Press. *Barbaro dies eight months after breakdown.* Retrieved from
http://msn.foxsports.com/horseracing/story/6421288?print=true

Associated Press. *Scholarship started in Barbaro's name.* Retrieved from
http://www.thehorse.com/PrintArticle.aspx?ID=8799

Associated Press. *Barbaro's legacy: Veterinary learning, public education, research
funding.* Retrieved from
http://www.thehorse.com/PrintArticle.aspx?ID=8843

Associated Press. *No sperm taken from euthanized Barbaro.* Retrieved from
http://www.msnbc.msn.com/id/16890406/print/1/displaymode/1098/

Associated Press. *Racing industry establishes Barbaro research fund.*
Retrieved from
http://www.msnbc.msn.com/id/16924626/print/1/displaymode/1098/

Associated Press. *Barbaro's siblings must carry on legacy.* Retrieved from
http://www.msnbc.msn.com/id/16909163/print/1/displaymode/1098/

Associated Press. *Barbaro euthanized after lengthy battle.* Retrieved from
http://www.msnbc.msn.com/id/16846723/print/1/displaymode/1098/

Associated Press. *Derby winner Barbaro 'doing better' vet says.* Retrieved from
http://www.foxnews.com/story/0,2933,203560,00.html

Barbaro Blood-Horse Citations

(2005) pp 6860, 6892 (2006) 630, 928,976, 2037,2090,2136,2433,2500, 2594, 2689, 2731, 2759, 2834, 2874, 2995, 3025, 3060, 3122, 3140, 3144, 3238, 3338, 3470, 3493, 3939, 4066, 7457, 7546. (2007) commemorative issue

Legacy Electronic Sources

Adams, K. *Old Friends gets TV exposure, retirement plan.* Retrieved from
http://www.bloodhorse.com/viewstory_plain.asp?id=39363

DeRosa, E. *Equine safety essential to ensuring fan confidence.* Retrieved from
http://www.thoroughbredtimes.com/news/printable.aspx

Duckworth, A. *Slaughter bills advancing in Congress.* Retrieved from
http://news.bloodhorse.com/viewstory.asp?id=38696

Gantz, T. *Cushion Track praised as Hollywood opens.* Retrieved from
http://www.bloodhorse.com/viewstory_plain.asp?id=36157

Hollywood Park enters new era with Cushion Track. Retrieved on June 14, 2007 from
http://www.hollywoodpark.com/bet_the_races/racing_news/racing_news_10272006.html

Horse rescue. Retrieved on July 8, 2007 from
http://www.timwoolleyracing.com/wiki/index.php/Horse_rescue

Kentucky Equine Humane Center officially opens. Retrieved on May 8, 2007 from
http://www/bloodhorse.com/viewstory_plain.asp?id=38477

Law, T. *New York franchise, synthetic surfaces discussed at Round Table.*
Retrieved from
http://www.thoroughbredtimes.com/news/printable.aspx

Lenz, T. *Commentary: Our responsibility.* Retrieved from
http://www.bloodhorse.com/viewstory_plain.asp?id=39424

McDonald, R. *Finding alternatives.* Retrieved from
http://www.bloodhorse.com/viewstory.asp?id=10535

Maine professor sets goal to make racetrack surfaces safer.
Retrieved on May 9, 2007 from
http://www.thoroughbredtimes.com/news/printable.aspx

Marr, E. *Woodbine has plan to address Polytrack problems.* Retrieved from
http://www.bloodhorse.com/viewstory_plain.asp?id=38288

New York horsemen and NYRA initiate Ferdinand fee to end horse slaughter.
Retrieved from
http://www.fund4horses.org/info.php?id+601

Nilsen, R. *The changing landscape – handicapping all-weather surfaces.*
Retrieved from
http://www.brisnet.com/cgibin/static.cgi?page=
TheChangingLandscapeHandicappingALL

Novak, C. *Kentucky Equine Humane Center draws interest.* Retrieved from
http://news.bloodhorse.com/viewstory.asp?id=39642

Paulick, R. *Death of a Derby winner: Slaughterhouse likely fate for Ferdinand.*
Retrieved from
http://news.bloodhorse.com/viewstory.asp?id=17051

Paulick, R. *Change of speed.* Retrieved from
http://www.bloodhorse.com/viewstory_plain.asp?id=38469

Synthetic track. Retrieved on May 24, 2007 from
http://www.timwoolleyracing.com/wiki/index.php/Synthetic_track

The Humane Society of the United States. *Get the facts on horse slaughter.*
Retrieved from
http://www.hsus.org/pet/issues_affecting_our_pets/equine
_protection/get_the_facts_on_h...

The Communication Alliance to network thoroughbred ex-racehorses. Retrieved from
http://www.canterusa.org/cwhatis.htm

Veterinarians for Equine Welfare. *Fact sheet: Transport to slaughter.* Retrieved from
http://www.vetsforequinewelfare.org/transport_slaughter.php

DVDs, Videos and Films

BARBARO: A nation's horse. (2007). NBS Universal, Inc.

Ruffian. (2007). ESPN.

Smarty Jones: A Pennsylvania champion. (2005). Big Picture Alliance.

Thoroughbred racing's greatest moments: 2004 The year in pictures. (2005). Horsephotos.

Photo Credits

Courtesy of Keeneland Library-Morgan Collection

Courtesy of Keeneland Library-Meadors Collection

NYRA-Courtesy of Bob Coglianese

Thoroughbred Times-William J. Stravitz

Photo courtesy of The State Museum of Pennsylvania, Don Giles, Photographer

Courtesy of Dell Hancock, Photographer

Photos by Z

Three Chimneys Farm

Michael Chapman

Deborah Given

Dan Farrell

Mike Bell

Laurie Johnson

Marie Shafer

Jennifer Duffy

mikewylot.com

Linda G. Hanna, Ed.D.

Artwork

Pierre E. Bellocq

Heather Rohde

Photo Arrangements

Linda G. Hanna, Ed. D. and Mark A. Dietzler

Barbaro, Smarty Jones and Ruffian